D1245910

THIS IS YOUR **PASSBOOK**® FOR ...

FOREMAN CARPENTER

NATIONAL LEARNING CORPORATION®
passbooks.com

Copyright © 2018 by

NLC®

National Learning Corporation

212 Michael Drive, Syosset, NY 11791
(516) 921-8888 • www.passbooks.com
E-mail: info@passbooks.com

PUBLISHED IN THE UNITED STATES OF AMERICA

PASSBOOK® SERIES

THE *PASSBOOK® SERIES* has been created to prepare applicants and candidates for the ultimate academic battlefield – the examination room.

At some time in our lives, each and every one of us may be required to take an examination – for validation, matriculation, admission, qualification, registration, certification, or licensure.

Based on the assumption that every applicant or candidate has met the basic formal educational standards, has taken the required number of courses, and read the necessary texts, the *PASSBOOK® SERIES* furnishes the one special preparation which may assure passing with confidence, instead of failing with insecurity. Examination questions – together with answers – are furnished as the basic vehicle for study so that the mysteries of the examination and its compounding difficulties may be eliminated or diminished by a sure method.

This book is meant to help you pass your examination provided that you qualify and are serious in your objective.

The entire field is reviewed through the huge store of content information which is succinctly presented through a provocative and challenging approach – the question-and-answer method.

A climate of success is established by furnishing the correct answers at the end of each test.

You soon learn to recognize types of questions, forms of questions, and patterns of questioning. You may even begin to anticipate expected outcomes.

You perceive that many questions are repeated or adapted so that you can gain acute insights, which may enable you to score many sure points.

You learn how to confront new questions, or types of questions, and to attack them confidently and work out the correct answers.

You note objectives and emphases, and recognize pitfalls and dangers, so that you may make positive educational adjustments.

Moreover, you are kept fully informed in relation to new concepts, methods, practices, and directions in the field.

You discover that you arre actually taking the examination all the time: you are preparing for the examination by "taking" an examination, not by reading extraneous and/or supererogatory textbooks.

In short, this PASSBOOK®, used directedly, should be an important factor in helping you to pass your test.

FOREMAN CARPENTER

DUTIES AND RESPONSIBILITIES
Under general direction, supervises, directs, and is responsible for the work of carpenters and other assigned employees; performs related work.

EXAMPLES OF TYPICAL TASKS
Assigns and lays out jobs for carpenters and closely allied workers; supervises, directs, and inspects the work of carpenters relating to the installation, alteration, and/or replacement of flooring, doors, building hardware, trim, window frames, sashes, partitions (dry wall and steel), etc.; estimates job requirements from plans and specifications and/or field surveys. Requisitions materials and equipment; supervises, directs, and is responsible for the proper operation and maintenance of the departmental carpentry shop(s); when required, lays out and supervises the heavy and rough carpentry work in the construction, maintenance, and repair of shoring, bulkheads, scaffolds, dock facilities, construction sheds, promenades, etc.; keeps records and prepares reports.

TESTS
The written test may include questions on supervisory and administrative procedures, including work assigning and coordinating, discipline, motivation, training, human relations, and understanding of printed matter; writing reports, forms, ordering of materials, record keeping, safety methods; carpentry, including work methods, types of tools, proper use of equipment, compliance with proper work procedures; estimating time, costs, and material; blueprint or plan reading, basic mathematical computations; and other related areas.

HOW TO TAKE A TEST

I. YOU MUST PASS AN EXAMINATION

A. *WHAT EVERY CANDIDATE SHOULD KNOW*

Examination applicants often ask us for help in preparing for the written test. What can I study in advance? What kinds of questions will be asked? How will the test be given? How will the papers be graded?

As an applicant for a civil service examination, you may be wondering about some of these things. Our purpose here is to suggest effective methods of advance study and to describe civil service examinations.

Your chances for success on this examination can be increased if you know how to prepare. Those "pre-examination jitters" can be reduced if you know what to expect. You can even experience an adventure in good citizenship if you know why civil service exams are given.

B. *WHY ARE CIVIL SERVICE EXAMINATIONS GIVEN?*

Civil service examinations are important to you in two ways. As a citizen, you want public jobs filled by employees who know how to do their work. As a job seeker, you want a fair chance to compete for that job on an equal footing with other candidates. The best-known means of accomplishing this two-fold goal is the competitive examination.

Exams are widely publicized throughout the nation. They may be administered for jobs in federal, state, city, municipal, town or village governments or agencies.

Any citizen may apply, with some limitations, such as the age or residence of applicants. Your experience and education may be reviewed to see whether you meet the requirements for the particular examination. When these requirements exist, they are reasonable and applied consistently to all applicants. Thus, a competitive examination may cause you some uneasiness now, but it is your privilege and safeguard.

C. *HOW ARE CIVIL SERVICE EXAMS DEVELOPED?*

Examinations are carefully written by trained technicians who are specialists in the field known as "psychological measurement," in consultation with recognized authorities in the field of work that the test will cover. These experts recommend the subject matter areas or skills to be tested; only those knowledges or skills important to your success on the job are included. The most reliable books and source materials available are used as references. Together, the experts and technicians judge the difficulty level of the questions.

Test technicians know how to phrase questions so that the problem is clearly stated. Their ethics do not permit "trick" or "catch" questions. Questions may have been tried out on sample groups, or subjected to statistical analysis, to determine their usefulness.

Written tests are often used in combination with performance tests, ratings of training and experience, and oral interviews. All of these measures combine to form the best-known means of finding the right person for the right job.

II. HOW TO PASS THE WRITTEN TEST

A. NATURE OF THE EXAMINATION

To prepare intelligently for civil service examinations, you should know how they differ from school examinations you have taken. In school you were assigned certain definite pages to read or subjects to cover. The examination questions were quite detailed and usually emphasized memory. Civil service exams, on the other hand, try to discover your present ability to perform the duties of a position, plus your potentiality to learn these duties. In other words, a civil service exam attempts to predict how successful you will be. Questions cover such a broad area that they cannot be as minute and detailed as school exam questions.

In the public service similar kinds of work, or positions, are grouped together in one "class." This process is known as *position-classification*. All the positions in a class are paid according to the salary range for that class. One class title covers all of these positions, and they are all tested by the same examination.

B. FOUR BASIC STEPS

1) Study the announcement

How, then, can you know what subjects to study? Our best answer is: "Learn as much as possible about the class of positions for which you've applied." The exam will test the knowledge, skills and abilities needed to do the work.

Your most valuable source of information about the position you want is the official exam announcement. This announcement lists the training and experience qualifications. Check these standards and apply only if you come reasonably close to meeting them.

The brief description of the position in the examination announcement offers some clues to the subjects which will be tested. Think about the job itself. Review the duties in your mind. Can you perform them, or are there some in which you are rusty? Fill in the blank spots in your preparation.

Many jurisdictions preview the written test in the exam announcement by including a section called "Knowledge and Abilities Required," "Scope of the Examination," or some similar heading. Here you will find out specifically what fields will be tested.

2) Review your own background

Once you learn in general what the position is all about, and what you need to know to do the work, ask yourself which subjects you already know fairly well and which need improvement. You may wonder whether to concentrate on improving your strong areas or on building some background in your fields of weakness. When the announcement has specified "some knowledge" or "considerable knowledge," or has used adjectives like "beginning principles of…" or "advanced … methods," you can get a clue as to the number and difficulty of questions to be asked in any given field. More questions, and hence broader coverage, would be included for those subjects which are more important in the work. Now weigh your strengths and weaknesses against the job requirements and prepare accordingly.

3) **Determine the level of the position**

Another way to tell how intensively you should prepare is to understand the level of the job for which you are applying. Is it the entering level? In other words, is this the position in which beginners in a field of work are hired? Or is it an intermediate or advanced level? Sometimes this is indicated by such words as "Junior" or "Senior" in the class title. Other jurisdictions use Roman numerals to designate the level – Clerk I, Clerk II, for example. The word "Supervisor" sometimes appears in the title. If the level is not indicated by the title, check the description of duties. Will you be working under very close supervision, or will you have responsibility for independent decisions in this work?

4) **Choose appropriate study materials**

Now that you know the subjects to be examined and the relative amount of each subject to be covered, you can choose suitable study materials. For beginning level jobs, or even advanced ones, if you have a pronounced weakness in some aspect of your training, read a modern, standard textbook in that field. Be sure it is up to date and has general coverage. Such books are normally available at your library, and the librarian will be glad to help you locate one. For entry-level positions, questions of appropriate difficulty are chosen – neither highly advanced questions, nor those too simple. Such questions require careful thought but not advanced training.

If the position for which you are applying is technical or advanced, you will read more advanced, specialized material. If you are already familiar with the basic principles of your field, elementary textbooks would waste your time. Concentrate on advanced textbooks and technical periodicals. Think through the concepts and review difficult problems in your field.

These are all general sources. You can get more ideas on your own initiative, following these leads. For example, training manuals and publications of the government agency which employs workers in your field can be useful, particularly for technical and professional positions. A letter or visit to the government department involved may result in more specific study suggestions, and certainly will provide you with a more definite idea of the exact nature of the position you are seeking.

III. KINDS OF TESTS

Tests are used for purposes other than measuring knowledge and ability to perform specified duties. For some positions, it is equally important to test ability to make adjustments to new situations or to profit from training. In others, basic mental abilities not dependent on information are essential. Questions which test these things may not appear as pertinent to the duties of the position as those which test for knowledge and information. Yet they are often highly important parts of a fair examination. For very general questions, it is almost impossible to help you direct your study efforts. What we can do is to point out some of the more common of these general abilities needed in public service positions and describe some typical questions.

1) General information

Broad, general information has been found useful for predicting job success in some kinds of work. This is tested in a variety of ways, from vocabulary lists to questions about current events. Basic background in some field of work, such as sociology or economics, may be sampled in a group of questions. Often these are principles which have become familiar to most persons through exposure rather than through formal training. It is difficult to advise you how to study for these questions; being alert to the world around you is our best suggestion.

2) Verbal ability

An example of an ability needed in many positions is verbal or language ability. Verbal ability is, in brief, the ability to use and understand words. Vocabulary and grammar tests are typical measures of this ability. Reading comprehension or paragraph interpretation questions are common in many kinds of civil service tests. You are given a paragraph of written material and asked to find its central meaning.

3) Numerical ability

Number skills can be tested by the familiar arithmetic problem, by checking paired lists of numbers to see which are alike and which are different, or by interpreting charts and graphs. In the latter test, a graph may be printed in the test booklet which you are asked to use as the basis for answering questions.

4) Observation

A popular test for law-enforcement positions is the observation test. A picture is shown to you for several minutes, then taken away. Questions about the picture test your ability to observe both details and larger elements.

5) Following directions

In many positions in the public service, the employee must be able to carry out written instructions dependably and accurately. You may be given a chart with several columns, each column listing a variety of information. The questions require you to carry out directions involving the information given in the chart.

6) Skills and aptitudes

Performance tests effectively measure some manual skills and aptitudes. When the skill is one in which you are trained, such as typing or shorthand, you can practice. These tests are often very much like those given in business school or high school courses. For many of the other skills and aptitudes, however, no short-time preparation can be made. Skills and abilities natural to you or that you have developed throughout your lifetime are being tested.

Many of the general questions just described provide all the data needed to answer the questions and ask you to use your reasoning ability to find the answers. Your best preparation for these tests, as well as for tests of facts and ideas, is to be at your physical and mental best. You, no doubt, have your own methods of getting into an exam-taking mood and keeping "in shape." The next section lists some ideas on this subject.

IV. KINDS OF QUESTIONS

Only rarely is the "essay" question, which you answer in narrative form, used in civil service tests. Civil service tests are usually of the short-answer type. Full instructions for answering these questions will be given to you at the examination. But in case this is your first experience with short-answer questions and separate answer sheets, here is what you need to know:

1) Multiple-choice Questions

Most popular of the short-answer questions is the "multiple choice" or "best answer" question. It can be used, for example, to test for factual knowledge, ability to solve problems or judgment in meeting situations found at work.

A multiple-choice question is normally one of three types—

- It can begin with an incomplete statement followed by several possible endings. You are to find the one ending which *best* completes the statement, although some of the others may not be entirely wrong.
- It can also be a complete statement in the form of a question which is answered by choosing one of the statements listed.
- It can be in the form of a problem – again you select the best answer.

Here is an example of a multiple-choice question with a discussion which should give you some clues as to the method for choosing the right answer:

When an employee has a complaint about his assignment, the action which will *best* help him overcome his difficulty is to
- A. discuss his difficulty with his coworkers
- B. take the problem to the head of the organization
- C. take the problem to the person who gave him the assignment
- D. say nothing to anyone about his complaint

In answering this question, you should study each of the choices to find which is best. Consider choice "A" – Certainly an employee may discuss his complaint with fellow employees, but no change or improvement can result, and the complaint remains unresolved. Choice "B" is a poor choice since the head of the organization probably does not know what assignment you have been given, and taking your problem to him is known as "going over the head" of the supervisor. The supervisor, or person who made the assignment, is the person who can clarify it or correct any injustice. Choice "C" is, therefore, correct. To say nothing, as in choice "D," is unwise. Supervisors have and interest in knowing the problems employees are facing, and the employee is seeking a solution to his problem.

2) True/False Questions

The "true/false" or "right/wrong" form of question is sometimes used. Here a complete statement is given. Your job is to decide whether the statement is right or wrong.

SAMPLE: A roaming cell-phone call to a nearby city costs less than a non-roaming call to a distant city.

This statement is wrong, or false, since roaming calls are more expensive.
This is not a complete list of all possible question forms, although most of the others are variations of these common types. You will always get complete directions for

answering questions. Be sure you understand *how* to mark your answers – ask questions until you do.

V. RECORDING YOUR ANSWERS

Computer terminals are used more and more today for many different kinds of exams.

For an examination with very few applicants, you may be told to record your answers in the test booklet itself. Separate answer sheets are much more common. If this separate answer sheet is to be scored by machine – and this is often the case – it is highly important that you mark your answers correctly in order to get credit.

An electronic scoring machine is often used in civil service offices because of the speed with which papers can be scored. Machine-scored answer sheets must be marked with a pencil, which will be given to you. This pencil has a high graphite content which responds to the electronic scoring machine. As a matter of fact, stray dots may register as answers, so do not let your pencil rest on the answer sheet while you are pondering the correct answer. Also, if your pencil lead breaks or is otherwise defective, ask for another.

Since the answer sheet will be dropped in a slot in the scoring machine, be careful not to bend the corners or get the paper crumpled.

The answer sheet normally has five vertical columns of numbers, with 30 numbers to a column. These numbers correspond to the question numbers in your test booklet. After each number, going across the page are four or five pairs of dotted lines. These short dotted lines have small letters or numbers above them. The first two pairs may also have a "T" or "F" above the letters. This indicates that the first two pairs only are to be used if the questions are of the true-false type. If the questions are multiple choice, disregard the "T" and "F" and pay attention only to the small letters or numbers.

Answer your questions in the manner of the sample that follows:

32. The largest city in the United States is
    A. Washington, D.C.
    B. New York City
    C. Chicago
    D. Detroit
    E. San Francisco

1) Choose the answer you think is best. (New York City is the largest, so "B" is correct.)
2) Find the row of dotted lines numbered the same as the question you are answering. (Find row number 32)
3) Find the pair of dotted lines corresponding to the answer. (Find the pair of lines under the mark "B.")
4) Make a solid black mark between the dotted lines.

VI. BEFORE THE TEST

Common sense will help you find procedures to follow to get ready for an examination. Too many of us, however, overlook these sensible measures. Indeed, nervousness and fatigue have been found to be the most serious reasons why applicants fail to do their best on civil service tests. Here is a list of reminders:

- Begin your preparation early – Don't wait until the last minute to go scurrying around for books and materials or to find out what the position is all about.
- Prepare continuously – An hour a night for a week is better than an all-night cram session. This has been definitely established. What is more, a night a week for a month will return better dividends than crowding your study into a shorter period of time.
- Locate the place of the exam – You have been sent a notice telling you when and where to report for the examination. If the location is in a different town or otherwise unfamiliar to you, it would be well to inquire the best route and learn something about the building.
- Relax the night before the test – Allow your mind to rest. Do not study at all that night. Plan some mild recreation or diversion; then go to bed early and get a good night's sleep.
- Get up early enough to make a leisurely trip to the place for the test – This way unforeseen events, traffic snarls, unfamiliar buildings, etc. will not upset you.
- Dress comfortably – A written test is not a fashion show. You will be known by number and not by name, so wear something comfortable.
- Leave excess paraphernalia at home – Shopping bags and odd bundles will get in your way. You need bring only the items mentioned in the official notice you received; usually everything you need is provided. Do not bring reference books to the exam. They will only confuse those last minutes and be taken away from you when in the test room.
- Arrive somewhat ahead of time – If because of transportation schedules you must get there very early, bring a newspaper or magazine to take your mind off yourself while waiting.
- Locate the examination room – When you have found the proper room, you will be directed to the seat or part of the room where you will sit. Sometimes you are given a sheet of instructions to read while you are waiting. Do not fill out any forms until you are told to do so; just read them and be prepared.
- Relax and prepare to listen to the instructions
- If you have any physical problem that may keep you from doing your best, be sure to tell the test administrator. If you are sick or in poor health, you really cannot do your best on the exam. You can come back and take the test some other time.

VII. AT THE TEST

The day of the test is here and you have the test booklet in your hand. The temptation to get going is very strong. Caution! There is more to success than knowing the right answers. You must know how to identify your papers and understand variations in the type of short-answer question used in this particular examination. Follow these suggestions for maximum results from your efforts:

1) Cooperate with the monitor

The test administrator has a duty to create a situation in which you can be as much at ease as possible. He will give instructions, tell you when to begin, check to see that you are marking your answer sheet correctly, and so on. He is not there to guard you, although he will see that your competitors do not take unfair advantage. He wants to help you do your best.

2) Listen to all instructions

Don't jump the gun! Wait until you understand all directions. In most civil service tests you get more time than you need to answer the questions. So don't be in a hurry. Read each word of instructions until you clearly understand the meaning. Study the examples, listen to all announcements and follow directions. Ask questions if you do not understand what to do.

3) Identify your papers

Civil service exams are usually identified by number only. You will be assigned a number; you must not put your name on your test papers. Be sure to copy your number correctly. Since more than one exam may be given, copy your exact examination title.

4) Plan your time

Unless you are told that a test is a "speed" or "rate of work" test, speed itself is usually not important. Time enough to answer all the questions will be provided, but this does not mean that you have all day. An overall time limit has been set. Divide the total time (in minutes) by the number of questions to determine the approximate time you have for each question.

5) Do not linger over difficult questions

If you come across a difficult question, mark it with a paper clip (useful to have along) and come back to it when you have been through the booklet. One caution if you do this – be sure to skip a number on your answer sheet as well. Check often to be sure that you have not lost your place and that you are marking in the row numbered the same as the question you are answering.

6) Read the questions

Be sure you know what the question asks! Many capable people are unsuccessful because they failed to *read* the questions correctly.

7) Answer all questions

Unless you have been instructed that a penalty will be deducted for incorrect answers, it is better to guess than to omit a question.

8) Speed tests

It is often better NOT to guess on speed tests. It has been found that on timed tests people are tempted to spend the last few seconds before time is called in marking answers at random – without even reading them – in the hope of picking up a few extra points. To discourage this practice, the instructions may warn you that your score will be "corrected" for guessing. That is, a penalty will be applied. The incorrect answers will be deducted from the correct ones, or some other penalty formula will be used.

9) Review your answers

If you finish before time is called, go back to the questions you guessed or omitted to give them further thought. Review other answers if you have time.

10) Return your test materials

If you are ready to leave before others have finished or time is called, take ALL your materials to the monitor and leave quietly. Never take any test material with you. The monitor can discover whose papers are not complete, and taking a test booklet may be grounds for disqualification.

VIII. EXAMINATION TECHNIQUES

1) Read the general instructions carefully. These are usually printed on the first page of the exam booklet. As a rule, these instructions refer to the timing of the examination; the fact that you should not start work until the signal and must stop work at a signal, etc. If there are any *special* instructions, such as a choice of questions to be answered, make sure that you note this instruction carefully.

2) When you are ready to start work on the examination, that is as soon as the signal has been given, read the instructions to each question booklet, underline any key words or phrases, such as *least*, *best*, *outline*, *describe* and the like. In this way you will tend to answer as requested rather than discover on reviewing your paper that you *listed without describing*, that you selected the *worst* choice rather than the *best* choice, etc.

3) If the examination is of the objective or multiple-choice type – that is, each question will also give a series of possible answers: A, B, C or D, and you are called upon to select the best answer and write the letter next to that answer on your answer paper – it is advisable to start answering each question in turn. There may be anywhere from 50 to 100 such questions in the three or four hours allotted and you can see how much time would be taken if you read through all the questions before beginning to answer any. Furthermore, if you come across a question or group of questions which you know would be difficult to answer, it would undoubtedly affect your handling of all the other questions.

4) If the examination is of the essay type and contains but a few questions, it is a moot point as to whether you should read all the questions before starting to answer any one. Of course, if you are given a choice – say five out of seven and the like – then it is essential to read all the questions so you can eliminate the two that are most difficult. If, however, you are asked to answer all the questions, there may be danger in trying to answer the easiest one first because you may find that you will spend too much time on it. The best technique is to answer the first question, then proceed to the second, etc.

5) Time your answers. Before the exam begins, write down the time it started, then add the time allowed for the examination and write down the time it must be completed, then divide the time available somewhat as follows:

- If 3-1/2 hours are allowed, that would be 210 minutes. If you have 80 objective-type questions, that would be an average of 2-1/2 minutes per question. Allow yourself no more than 2 minutes per question, or a total of 160 minutes, which will permit about 50 minutes to review.
- If for the time allotment of 210 minutes there are 7 essay questions to answer, that would average about 30 minutes a question. Give yourself only 25 minutes per question so that you have about 35 minutes to review.

6) The most important instruction is to *read each question* and make sure you know what is wanted. The second most important instruction is to *time yourself properly* so that you answer every question. The third most important instruction is to *answer every question.* Guess if you have to but include something for each question. Remember that you will receive no credit for a blank and will probably receive some credit if you write something in answer to an essay question. If you guess a letter – say "B" for a multiple-choice question – you may have guessed right. If you leave a blank as an answer to a multiple-choice question, the examiners may respect your feelings but it will not add a point to your score. Some exams may penalize you for wrong answers, so in such cases *only,* you may not want to guess unless you have some basis for your answer.

7) Suggestions
   a. Objective-type questions
      1. Examine the question booklet for proper sequence of pages and questions
      2. Read all instructions carefully
      3. Skip any question which seems too difficult; return to it after all other questions have been answered
      4. Apportion your time properly; do not spend too much time on any single question or group of questions
      5. Note and underline key words – *all, most, fewest, least, best, worst, same, opposite,* etc.
      6. Pay particular attention to negatives
      7. Note unusual option, e.g., unduly long, short, complex, different or similar in content to the body of the question
      8. Observe the use of "hedging" words – *probably, may, most likely,* etc.
      9. Make sure that your answer is put next to the same number as the question
      10. Do not second-guess unless you have good reason to believe the second answer is definitely more correct
      11. Cross out original answer if you decide another answer is more accurate; do not erase until you are ready to hand your paper in
      12. Answer all questions; guess unless instructed otherwise
      13. Leave time for review

   b. Essay questions
      1. Read each question carefully
      2. Determine exactly what is wanted. Underline key words or phrases.
      3. Decide on outline or paragraph answer

4. Include many different points and elements unless asked to develop any one or two points or elements
5. Show impartiality by giving pros and cons unless directed to select one side only
6. Make and write down any assumptions you find necessary to answer the questions
7. Watch your English, grammar, punctuation and choice of words
8. Time your answers; don't crowd material

8) Answering the essay question

Most essay questions can be answered by framing the specific response around several key words or ideas. Here are a few such key words or ideas:

M's: manpower, materials, methods, money, management
P's: purpose, program, policy, plan, procedure, practice, problems, pitfalls, personnel, public relations
   a. Six basic steps in handling problems:
      1. Preliminary plan and background development
      2. Collect information, data and facts
      3. Analyze and interpret information, data and facts
      4. Analyze and develop solutions as well as make recommendations
      5. Prepare report and sell recommendations
      6. Install recommendations and follow up effectiveness

   b. Pitfalls to avoid
      1. *Taking things for granted* – A statement of the situation does not necessarily imply that each of the elements is necessarily true; for example, a complaint may be invalid and biased so that all that can be taken for granted is that a complaint has been registered
      2. *Considering only one side of a situation* – Wherever possible, indicate several alternatives and then point out the reasons you selected the best one
      3. *Failing to indicate follow up* – Whenever your answer indicates action on your part, make certain that you will take proper follow-up action to see how successful your recommendations, procedures or actions turn out to be
      4. *Taking too long in answering any single question* – Remember to time your answers properly

IX. AFTER THE TEST

Scoring procedures differ in detail among civil service jurisdictions although the general principles are the same. Whether the papers are hand-scored or graded by machine we have described, they are nearly always graded by number. That is, the person who marks the paper knows only the number – never the name – of the applicant. Not until all the papers have been graded will they be matched with names. If other tests, such as training and experience or oral interview ratings have been given, scores will be combined. Different parts of the examination usually have different weights. For example, the written test might count 60 percent of the final grade, and a rating of training and experience 40 percent. In many jurisdictions, veterans will have a certain number of points added to their grades.

After the final grade has been determined, the names are placed in grade order and an eligible list is established. There are various methods for resolving ties between those who get the same final grade – probably the most common is to place first the name of the person whose application was received first. Job offers are made from the eligible list in the order the names appear on it. You will be notified of your grade and your rank as soon as all these computations have been made. This will be done as rapidly as possible.

People who are found to meet the requirements in the announcement are called "eligibles." Their names are put on a list of eligible candidates. An eligible's chances of getting a job depend on how high he stands on this list and how fast agencies are filling jobs from the list.

When a job is to be filled from a list of eligibles, the agency asks for the names of people on the list of eligibles for that job. When the civil service commission receives this request, it sends to the agency the names of the three people highest on this list. Or, if the job to be filled has specialized requirements, the office sends the agency the names of the top three persons who meet these requirements from the general list.

The appointing officer makes a choice from among the three people whose names were sent to him. If the selected person accepts the appointment, the names of the others are put back on the list to be considered for future openings.

That is the rule in hiring from all kinds of eligible lists, whether they are for typist, carpenter, chemist, or something else. For every vacancy, the appointing officer has his choice of any one of the top three eligibles on the list. This explains why the person whose name is on top of the list sometimes does not get an appointment when some of the persons lower on the list do. If the appointing officer chooses the second or third eligible, the No. 1 eligible does not get a job at once, but stays on the list until he is appointed or the list is terminated.

X. HOW TO PASS THE INTERVIEW TEST

The examination for which you applied requires an oral interview test. You have already taken the written test and you are now being called for the interview test – the final part of the formal examination.

You may think that it is not possible to prepare for an interview test and that there are no procedures to follow during an interview. Our purpose is to point out some things you can do in advance that will help you and some good rules to follow and pitfalls to avoid while you are being interviewed.

What is an interview supposed to test?

The written examination is designed to test the technical knowledge and competence of the candidate; the oral is designed to evaluate intangible qualities, not readily measured otherwise, and to establish a list showing the relative fitness of each candidate – as measured against his competitors – for the position sought. Scoring is not on the basis of "right" and "wrong," but on a sliding scale of values ranging from "not passable" to "outstanding." As a matter of fact, it is possible to achieve a relatively low score without a single "incorrect" answer because of evident weakness in the qualities being measured.

Occasionally, an examination may consist entirely of an oral test – either an individual or a group oral. In such cases, information is sought concerning the technical knowledges and abilities of the candidate, since there has been no written examination for this purpose. More commonly, however, an oral test is used to supplement a written examination.

Who conducts interviews?

The composition of oral boards varies among different jurisdictions. In nearly all, a representative of the personnel department serves as chairman. One of the members of the board may be a representative of the department in which the candidate would work. In some cases, "outside experts" are used, and, frequently, a businessman or some other representative of the general public is asked to serve. Labor and management or other special groups may be represented. The aim is to secure the services of experts in the appropriate field.

However the board is composed, it is a good idea (and not at all improper or unethical) to ascertain in advance of the interview who the members are and what groups they represent. When you are introduced to them, you will have some idea of their backgrounds and interests, and at least you will not stutter and stammer over their names.

What should be done before the interview?

While knowledge about the board members is useful and takes some of the surprise element out of the interview, there is other preparation which is more substantive. It *is* possible to prepare for an oral interview – in several ways:

1) Keep a copy of your application and review it carefully before the interview

This may be the only document before the oral board, and the starting point of the interview. Know what education and experience you have listed there, and the sequence and dates of all of it. Sometimes the board will ask you to review the highlights of your experience for them; you should not have to hem and haw doing it.

2) Study the class specification and the examination announcement

Usually, the oral board has one or both of these to guide them. The qualities, characteristics or knowledges required by the position sought are stated in these documents. They offer valuable clues as to the nature of the oral interview. For example, if the job involves supervisory responsibilities, the announcement will usually indicate that knowledge of modern supervisory methods and the qualifications of the candidate as a supervisor will be tested. If so, you can expect such questions, frequently in the form of a hypothetical situation which you are expected to solve. NEVER go into an oral without knowledge of the duties and responsibilities of the job you seek.

3) Think through each qualification required

Try to visualize the kind of questions you would ask if you were a board member. How well could you answer them? Try especially to appraise your own knowledge and background in each area, *measured against the job sought*, and identify any areas in which you are weak. Be critical and realistic – do not flatter yourself.

14

4) Do some general reading in areas in which you feel you may be weak

For example, if the job involves supervision and your past experience has NOT, some general reading in supervisory methods and practices, particularly in the field of human relations, might be useful. Do NOT study agency procedures or detailed manuals. The oral board will be testing your understanding and capacity, not your memory.

5) Get a good night's sleep and watch your general health and mental attitude

You will want a clear head at the interview. Take care of a cold or any other minor ailment, and of course, no hangovers.

What should be done on the day of the interview?

Now comes the day of the interview itself. Give yourself plenty of time to get there. Plan to arrive somewhat ahead of the scheduled time, particularly if your appointment is in the fore part of the day. If a previous candidate fails to appear, the board might be ready for you a bit early. By early afternoon an oral board is almost invariably behind schedule if there are many candidates, and you may have to wait. Take along a book or magazine to read, or your application to review, but leave any extraneous material in the waiting room when you go in for your interview. In any event, relax and compose yourself.

The matter of dress is important. The board is forming impressions about you – from your experience, your manners, your attitude, and your appearance. Give your personal appearance careful attention. Dress your best, but not your flashiest. Choose conservative, appropriate clothing, and be sure it is immaculate. This is a business interview, and your appearance should indicate that you regard it as such. Besides, being well groomed and properly dressed will help boost your confidence.

Sooner or later, someone will call your name and escort you into the interview room. *This is it.* From here on you are on your own. It is too late for any more preparation. But remember, you asked for this opportunity to prove your fitness, and you are here because your request was granted.

What happens when you go in?

The usual sequence of events will be as follows: The clerk (who is often the board stenographer) will introduce you to the chairman of the oral board, who will introduce you to the other members of the board. Acknowledge the introductions before you sit down. Do not be surprised if you find a microphone facing you or a stenotypist sitting by. Oral interviews are usually recorded in the event of an appeal or other review.

Usually the chairman of the board will open the interview by reviewing the highlights of your education and work experience from your application – primarily for the benefit of the other members of the board, as well as to get the material into the record. Do not interrupt or comment unless there is an error or significant misinterpretation; if that is the case, do not hesitate. But do not quibble about insignificant matters. Also, he will usually ask you some question about your education, experience or your present job – partly to get you to start talking and to establish the interviewing "rapport." He may start the actual questioning, or turn it over to one of the other members. Frequently, each member undertakes the questioning on a particular area, one in which he is perhaps most competent, so you can expect each member to participate in the examination. Because time is limited, you may also expect some rather abrupt switches in the direction the questioning takes, so do not be upset by it. Normally, a board member will not pursue a single line of questioning unless he discovers a particular strength or weakness.

After each member has participated, the chairman will usually ask whether any member has any further questions, then will ask you if you have anything you wish to add. Unless you are expecting this question, it may floor you. Worse, it may start you off on an extended, extemporaneous speech. The board is not usually seeking more information. The question is principally to offer you a last opportunity to present further qualifications or to indicate that you have nothing to add. So, if you feel that a significant qualification or characteristic has been overlooked, it is proper to point it out in a sentence or so. Do not compliment the board on the thoroughness of their examination – they have been sketchy, and you know it. If you wish, merely say, "No thank you, I have nothing further to add." This is a point where you can "talk yourself out" of a good impression or fail to present an important bit of information. Remember, *you close the interview yourself.*

The chairman will then say, "That is all, Mr. _____, thank you." Do not be startled; the interview is over, and quicker than you think. Thank him, gather your belongings and take your leave. Save your sigh of relief for the other side of the door.

How to put your best foot forward
Throughout this entire process, you may feel that the board individually and collectively is trying to pierce your defenses, seek out your hidden weaknesses and embarrass and confuse you. Actually, this is not true. They are obliged to make an appraisal of your qualifications for the job you are seeking, and they want to see you in your best light. Remember, they must interview all candidates and a non-cooperative candidate may become a failure in spite of their best efforts to bring out his qualifications. Here are 15 suggestions that will help you:

1) Be natural – Keep your attitude confident, not cocky
If you are not confident that you can do the job, do not expect the board to be. Do not apologize for your weaknesses, try to bring out your strong points. The board is interested in a positive, not negative, presentation. Cockiness will antagonize any board member and make him wonder if you are covering up a weakness by a false show of strength.

2) Get comfortable, but don't lounge or sprawl
Sit erectly but not stiffly. A careless posture may lead the board to conclude that you are careless in other things, or at least that you are not impressed by the importance of the occasion. Either conclusion is natural, even if incorrect. Do not fuss with your clothing, a pencil or an ashtray. Your hands may occasionally be useful to emphasize a point; do not let them become a point of distraction.

3) Do not wisecrack or make small talk
This is a serious situation, and your attitude should show that you consider it as such. Further, the time of the board is limited – they do not want to waste it, and neither should you.

4) Do not exaggerate your experience or abilities
In the first place, from information in the application or other interviews and sources, the board may know more about you than you think. Secondly, you probably will not get away with it. An experienced board is rather adept at spotting such a situation, so do not take the chance.

5) If you know a board member, do not make a point of it, yet do not hide it

Certainly you are not fooling him, and probably not the other members of the board. Do not try to take advantage of your acquaintanceship – it will probably do you little good.

6) Do not dominate the interview

Let the board do that. They will give you the clues – do not assume that you have to do all the talking. Realize that the board has a number of questions to ask you, and do not try to take up all the interview time by showing off your extensive knowledge of the answer to the first one.

7) Be attentive

You only have 20 minutes or so, and you should keep your attention at its sharpest throughout. When a member is addressing a problem or question to you, give him your undivided attention. Address your reply principally to him, but do not exclude the other board members.

8) Do not interrupt

A board member may be stating a problem for you to analyze. He will ask you a question when the time comes. Let him state the problem, and wait for the question.

9) Make sure you understand the question

Do not try to answer until you are sure what the question is. If it is not clear, restate it in your own words or ask the board member to clarify it for you. However, do not haggle about minor elements.

10) Reply promptly but not hastily

A common entry on oral board rating sheets is "candidate responded readily," or "candidate hesitated in replies." Respond as promptly and quickly as you can, but do not jump to a hasty, ill-considered answer.

11) Do not be peremptory in your answers

A brief answer is proper – but do not fire your answer back. That is a losing game from your point of view. The board member can probably ask questions much faster than you can answer them.

12) Do not try to create the answer you think the board member wants

He is interested in what kind of mind you have and how it works – not in playing games. Furthermore, he can usually spot this practice and will actually grade you down on it.

13) Do not switch sides in your reply merely to agree with a board member

Frequently, a member will take a contrary position merely to draw you out and to see if you are willing and able to defend your point of view. Do not start a debate, yet do not surrender a good position. If a position is worth taking, it is worth defending.

14) Do not be afraid to admit an error in Judgment if you are shown to be wrong

The board knows that you are forced to reply without any opportunity for careful consideration. Your answer may be demonstrably wrong. If so, admit it and get on with the interview.

15) Do not dwell at length on your present job

The opening question may relate to your present assignment. Answer the question but do not go into an extended discussion. You are being examined for a *new* job, not your present one. As a matter of fact, try to phrase ALL your answers in terms of the job for which you are being examined.

Basis of Rating

Probably you will forget most of these "do's" and "don'ts" when you walk into the oral interview room. Even remembering them all will not ensure you a passing grade. Perhaps you did not have the qualifications in the first place. But remembering them will help you to put your best foot forward, without treading on the toes of the board members.

Rumor and popular opinion to the contrary notwithstanding, an oral board wants you to make the best appearance possible. They know you are under pressure – but they also want to see how you respond to it as a guide to what your reaction would be under the pressures of the job you seek. They will be influenced by the degree of poise you display, the personal traits you show and the manner in which you respond.

ABOUT THIS BOOK

This book contains tests divided into Examination Sections. Go through each test, answering every question in the margin. At the end of each test look at the answer key and check your answers. On the ones you got wrong, look at the right answer choice and learn. Do not fill in the answers first. Do not memorize the questions and answers, but understand the answer and principles involved. On your test, the questions will likely be different from the samples. Questions are changed and new ones added. If you understand these past questions you should have success with any changes that arise. Tests may consist of several types of questions. We have additional books on each subject should more study be advisable or necessary for you. Finally, the more you study, the better prepared you will be. This book is intended to be the last thing you study before you walk into the examination room. Prior study of relevant texts is also recommended. NLC publishes some of these in our Fundamental Series. Knowledge and good sense are important factors in passing your exam. Good luck also helps. So now study this Passbook, absorb the material contained within and take that knowledge into the examination. Then do your best to pass that exam.

———

EXAMINATION SECTION

EXAMINATION SECTION
TEST 1

DIRECTIONS: Each question or incomplete statement is followed by several suggested answers or completions. Select the one that BEST answers the question or completes the statement. *PRINT THE LETTER OF THE CORRECT ANSWER IN THE SPACE AT THE RIGHT.*

1. If a new structural maintenance procedure has been adopted, the gang foreman should keep this work under his close supervision until the procedure has become routine. The MOST important reason for doing this is to 1.____

    A. prevent the men from criticizing the procedure
    B. make certain that the men are acquainted with all the details
    C. get the work done as quickly as possible
    D. impress the men with the importance of the job

2. A gang foreman should presume that the MOST likely reason for a new worker to experience difficulty when he is learning his job is that he 2.____

    A. wants to pick it up in his own way
    B. is nervous and lacks confidence in himself
    C. has no desire to learn
    D. has no respect for this gang foreman

3. The MOST important thing for a gang foreman to bear in mind in trying to establish a good safety record is that 3.____

    A. a certain number of accidents will happen to his men, according to the law of averages, regardless of the precautions taken
    B. a way can be found to prevent most accidents
    C. certain individuals who are accident-prone will defeat all measures taken to protect them
    D. some accidents are unavoidable if production is to be maintained at the required level

4. Concrete platforms are finished off with wooden edging strips. This design feature is of interest to the maintenance of way department because these strips 4.____

    A. perform a useful function under emergency conditions
    B. serve as markers to outline the platform edge
    C. are easier and less costly to maintain than a concrete edge
    D. make a more durable edge than concrete

5. In order to select a bit to drill a 5/8" hole from a set of auger bits, you SHOULD 5.____

    A. look for one marked 5/8" on the shank
    B. check diameters with a caliper set at 5/8"
    C. look for one marked 10 on the tang
    D. pick out the likely one by eye and check size by a test hole in a scrap piece of wood

6. A number of different woods are used for fine interior finishes. However, a wood which would most likely NOT be used for this purpose is   6.____

    A. birch   B. chestnut   C. red gum   D. ash

7. The cleats that are fastened to the sides of a girder to help support the joists that frame into it are called   7.____

    A. ledger boards   B. cripples
    C. verge boards   D. toe-holts

8. By rotating the work assignments of his men, a gang foreman can expect to develop   8.____

    A. more useful men
    B. high individual output
    C. more speed on a particular job
    D. better quality of work on a particular job

9. There would MOST probably be poor morale in a gang of men whose gang foreman   9.____

    A. does not plan the work properly
    B. refuses to grant any special privileges
    C. insists on good housekeeping
    D. enforces the rules and regulations

10. When instructing newly appointed helpers in the duties pertaining to structure mainte-nance work, a gang foreman should NOT   10.____

    A. talk slowly
    B. take too much for granted
    C. refer to work done by maintainers
    D. permit them to ask questions *after* he has finished

11. A good first aid treatment to administer to a man who has apparently been rendered unconscious by a high voltage shock would be to   11.____

    A. give him a stimulant by mouth
    B. apply artificial respiration if he is not breathing
    C. apply artificial respiration as a precautionary measure even if he is breathing
    D. keep him warm and comfortable

12. A two-foot-long carpenter's level was used to check a wood sill on top of one side of a concrete foundation wall. The sill was found to be out of level by 1/8".
If the length of the sill was 30'6", the sill would have to be shimmed a MAXIMUM amount of *approximately*   12.____

    A. 1/8"   B. 3/4"   C. 1 7/8"   D. 3 3/4"

13. A price inquiry was made of two lumberyards on 100 2 x 4's 10 feet and 100 2 x 10's 12 feet. Yard A quoted a price of 10¢ per lineal foot for the 2 x 4's and 25¢ per lineal foot for the 2 x 10's. Yard B quoted a price of 15¢ per board-foot for both items.
It can, therefore, be calculated that the price of Yard A is   13.____

    A. cheaper than Yard B for the 2 x 4's but dearer for the 2 x 10's
    B. dearer than Yard B for the 2 x 4's but cheaper for the 2 x 10's

C.   the same as Yard B for the 2 x 4's but dearer for the 2 x 10's
D.   the same as Yard B for both items

14.   The nail-holding power of hardwoods, compared to that of softwoods, is   14._____

A.   about double
B.   about the same
C.   about one-half
D.   greater or smaller, depending on the particular species being compared

15.   A gang foreman arranging for the delivery of material and equipment to a job would NOT   15._____
specify

A.   whether the delivery should be made by work train or truck
B.   the location to which the delivery is to be made
C.   when the delivery should be made
D.   the manner in which the material and equipment should be loaded for delivery

16.   Suppose that jobs under your supervision are sometimes delayed because the men   16._____
await your arrival to make decisions before proceeding with the work.
As a gang foreman, the MOST helpful conclusion you could draw from this condition is
that

A.   you have incurred the men's dislike
B.   the men under your supervision lack initiative and need encouragement
C.   the jobs assigned to your gang are generally more difficult than the average
D.   your orders and instructions may not have been sufficiently clear or complete

17.   If you detect an error in an order issued to you by your superior, you should   17._____

A.   try to carry out the order as issued because that is your duty
B.   point out the error to your superior because it is probably an oversight
C.   correct the error yourself and carry out the corrected order since this is your pre-
rogative as a gang foreman
D.   put the order aside until your superior detects and corrects the order himself

18.   A contributing cause present in practically all accidents is   18._____

A.   failure to give close attention to the job at hand
B.   lack of cooperation among the men in a gang
C.   failure to place the right man in the right job
D.   use of improper tools

19.   The sizes of hand saws which make up the MOST useful combination for general car-   19._____
pentry work are the _____ crosscut and the _____ rip.

A.   16-inch, 10-point; 24-inch, 10-point
B.   20-inch, 10-point; 26-inch, 8-point
C.   22-inch, 9-point; 20-inch, 9-point
D.   26-inch, 8-point; 26-inch, 5 1/2-point

20. A 3" x 6" timber used as a beam between supports 12 feet apart will safely support a uniform load of 80 pounds per lineal foot. 20.____
    If the same beam is used between supports which are only 6 feet apart, the uniform load per lineal foot can safely be INCREASED by _____ pounds.

    A. 80   B. 160   C. 240   D. 320

21. A gang foreman can BEST help to get a special rush job completed by 21.____

    A. permitting his men to ignore minor safety rules
    B. staying away while the job is being done
    C. making sure that all necessary tools and materials are on hand
    D. promising his men special favors for finishing on time

22. If the subfloor is laid diagonally, the finish flooring can be laid parallel to either dimension 22.____
    of the room because the

    A. finish floor will have a stronger foundation
    B. shrinkage of the subfloor will not noticeably affect the finish floor
    C. irregularities of the subfloor will then be equalized
    D. shrinkage of the subfloor will help pull the finish flooring together

23. A maintainer requests a special privilege because of certain unusual circumstances, and 23.____
    his gang foreman grants the request because he feels it to be definitely justified. Shortly
    thereafter, a helper requests the same privilege and gives as his only reason the fact that
    the maintainer had been granted this privilege.
    The gang foreman should, in the helper's case,

    A. grant the request because all men should be treated the same regardless of title
    B. grant the request to avoid a charge of discrimination against helpers
    C. deny the request and explain why it was granted to the maintainer
    D. tell him that the request will be granted if a better reason is furnished

24. A good principle to follow after teaching a structural procedure to one of your new men 24.____
    is to

    A. tell him you expect he will make many mistakes at first
    B. assume he knows the procedure if he has no questions to ask
    C. have him write out the procedure from memory
    D. observe his subsequent procedure and point out any errors he makes

25. Safety requires that wood ladders be unpainted. The PROBABLE reason for this is that 25.____
    paint

    A. is inflammable
    B. may deteriorate wood
    C. makes ladder rungs slippery
    D. may cover cracks or defects

KEY (CORRECT ANSWERS)

1.	B		11.	B
2.	B		12.	C
3.	B		13.	D
4.	C		14.	A
5.	C		15.	D
6.	D		16.	D
7.	A		17.	B
8.	A		18.	A
9.	A		19.	D
10.	B		20.	C

21.	C
22.	B
23.	C
24.	D
25.	D

TEST 2

DIRECTIONS: Each question or incomplete statement is followed by several suggested answers or completions. Select the one that BEST answers the question or completes the statement. *PRINT THE LETTER OF THE CORRECT ANSWER IN THE SPACE AT THE RIGHT.*

1. Two long boards are to be glued together, edge to edge. The two edges are BEST trued-up by the use of a _____ plane.

   A. block   B. smoothing   C. jack   D. fore

1.___

Questions 2-7.

DIRECTIONS: Questions 2 to 7, inclusive, are based on the sketch below representing the floor plan of a one-story frame structure. Consult this drawing when answering these questions.

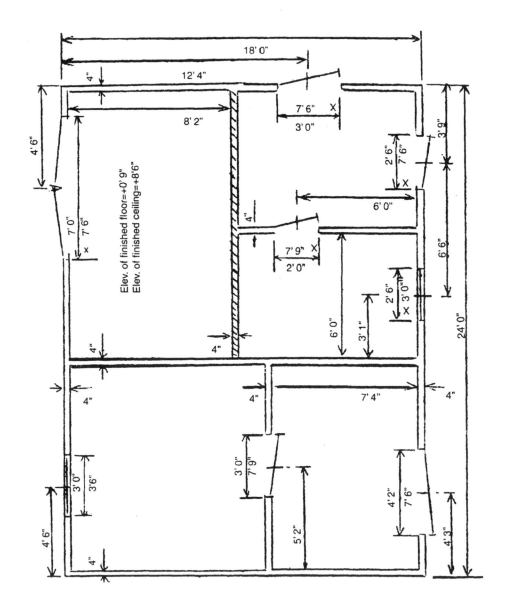

2. The number of linear feet of interior partitions required will be MOST NEARLY   2._____

    A. 44'2"   B. 46'6"   C. 49'2"   D. 51'6"

3. The total area of exterior openings, in square feet, will be MOST NEARLY   3._____

    A. 125   B. 143   C. 164   D. 182

4. The total exterior perimeter of the building, exclusive of door openings, will be MOST NEARLY   4._____

    A. 54'0"   B. 61'10"   C. 67'4"   D. 84'0"

5. The net floor area of the only corner room not provided with an exterior door is about _____ square feet.   5._____

    A. 53   B. 59   C. 97   D. 106

6. The dimensions of the LARGEST room are   6._____

    A. 9'8" x 13'0"   B. 8'2" x 13'0"
    C. 8'10" x 13'0"   D. 10'0" x 17'4"

7. If 2" x 3" studs are placed at 14" o.c., the cross-hatched interior partition will require _____ studs.   7._____

    A. 10   B. 11   C. 12   D. 13

8. If a gang foreman finds that he very frequently has to bring different members of his gang up for disciplinary action, he should   8._____

    A. realize that he has a gang of troublemakers on his hands
    B. ask the union delegate to take action
    C. ask to be transferred to a less troublesome group
    D. appraise and correct his errors in supervision

9. A gang foreman finds that his foreman, because of a personal problem, cannot concentrate sufficiently on his work to make decisions affecting the gang foreman's work assignments.
Of the following, the BEST immediate action for the gang foreman to take is to   9._____

    A. discuss the matter with other gang foremen under the foreman's supervision
    B. go to higher supervision for these decisions
    C. suggest appropriate decisions to his foreman and secure his approval for them
    D. be persistent in his requests to his foreman for the necessary decisions

10. If you notice one of your helpers doing a job in an unsafe manner and he tells you that this is the way the maintainer told him to do it, you should FIRST   10._____

    A. speak to this maintainer and find out if the helper was telling you the truth
    B. reprimand the helper for violating safety rules
    C. question this maintainer to see if he knows the safe way to do the job
    D. show the helper the correct method and see that he does the job properly

11. When filing saw teeth, it should be kept in mind that 　　　　11._____

    A. a rip saw is filed straight across but a crosscut saw is filed at a 45° angle
    B. both rip saws and crosscut saws are filed straight across
    C. a rip saw is filed at a 45° angle but a crosscut saw is filed straight across
    D. both rip saws and crosscut saws are filed at a 45° angle

12. Unless otherwise specified, finish flooring will be supplied *standard matched.*
    This means that the 　　　　12._____

    A. distance from the top surface to the center of the tongue and groove is greater than the distance from the bottom surface to this center
    B. distance from the top surface to the center of the tongue and groove is less than the distance from the bottom surface to this center
    C. flooring is flat-grain and the grain is matched within prescribed limits
    D. flooring is edge-grain and the grain is in the same direction through each piece of flooring

13. The MOST important reason for the use of furring on masonry surfaces is to provide 　　　　13._____

    A. a backing on which to nail lath
    B. a space for electric wiring
    C. thermal insulation
    D. increased structural strength for the finished plastered surface

14. If the drawing of a carpentry detail is made to a scale of 3/4" to the foot, a scaled measurement of 6" would represent a length of 　　　　14._____

    A. 3/8 inches   B. 8 inches   C. 4 1/2 feet   D. 8 feet

15. When the end of a wood joist is set in a brick wall, it should be 　　　　15._____

    A. cut on a bevel   B. set on a pilaster
    C. cut square   D. set on a corbel

16. If a person has a deep puncture in his finger caused by a sharp nail, the BEST immediate first aid procedure would be to 　　　　16._____

    A. encourage bleeding by exerting pressure around the injured area
    B. stop all bleeding
    C. prevent air from reaching the wound
    D. probe the wound for steel particles

17. The action MOST likely to increase the esteem of the men for their gang foreman would be for him to 　　　　17._____

    A. observe the same rules of conduct that he expects his men to observe
    B. expect all his men to perform with equal efficiency any jobs assigned to them
    C. always be frank and outspoken to his men in pointing out their faults
    D. interchange advice on personal problems with his men

18. A rectangular form can be checked for squareness by taking the necessary measurements using only a tape, or by checking the necessary number of corners using only a steel square, or by taking certain measurements with a tape combined with the checking of certain corners with a steel square.
The form CANNOT be correctly checked by using a

    A. tape and finding the opposite sides equal and the diagonals of the same length
    B. steel square and finding that three corners are each 90°
    C. steel square and finding that two diagonally opposite corners are each 90°
    D. tape and finding the opposite sides equal, then using a steel square and finding one corner is 90°

18._____

19. With respect to shrinking and swelling of wood, it is NOT true that

    A. wood which shrinks considerably upon drying will swell considerably when moistened
    B. a flat-grain board will shrink more in width than an edge-grain board
    C. settlement occurring in a building where studs are supported on top of joists is due to shrinkage in the studs
    D. any beam will shrink more in depth than in length

19._____

20. A foreman assigns a gang foreman to supervise a job which must be completed at the end of seven working days. The gang foreman has eight maintainers in his gang. At the end of three working days, although the work has been efficiently done, the job is only one-third completed. In order to complete the job on time, without overtime, the gang foreman should request that he be given _____ more maintainers.

    A. 3   B. 4   C. 5   D. 6

20._____

21. An IMPORTANT reason for installing grounds is to

    A. provide a dead air space for better heat insulation
    B. get a tight joint between the back of the interior trim and the finished plaster
    C. prevent chipping of the finished plaster surface
    D. give increased structural support for the finished plastered surface

21._____

22. When it is necessary to install rows of cross-bridging between floor joists, it is good practice to make the distance between the rows *no more than* _____ feet.

    A. 4   B. 8   C. 12   D. 16

22._____

23. It is MOST important to give complete details of an accident on the accident report because this will

    A. cause the injured employee to be more careful in the future
    B. keep supervision informed of the working conditions
    C. help in the defense against spurious compensation claims
    D. provide information to help avoid future accidents

23._____

9

24. An adjustable bit gauge will COMMONLY be used on an auger bit to   24.____
   A. countersink the holes
   B. obtain equal diameter holes
   C. eliminate the need for center punching
   D. drill a number of holes to the same depth

25. If a certain type of structural timber is said to have a factor of safety of 4, it means that   25.____
   A. it should be used to carry no more than one-fourth of its design load
   B. it can safely carry four times its design load
   C. only one-quarter of the ultimate strength of a perfect piece is used for design purposes
   D. it is four times as strong as any other type of structural timber

---

KEY (CORRECT ANSWERS)

1.	D	11.	A
2.	A	12.	A
3.	B	13.	A
4.	C	14.	D
5.	C	15.	A
6.	B	16.	A
7.	C	17.	A
8.	D	18.	C
9.	C	19.	C
10.	D	20.	B

21.	B
22.	B
23.	D
24.	D
25.	C

EXAMINATION SECTION
TEST 1

DIRECTIONS: Each question or incomplete statement is followed by several suggested answers or completions. Select the one that BEST answers the question or completes the statement. *PRINT THE LETTER OF THE CORRECT ANSWER IN THE SPACE AT THE RIGHT.*

1. A lintel is MOST closely associated with a   1._____
   - A. wall opening
   - B. floor opening
   - C. roof opening
   - D. fire escape

2. An apron is MOST closely associated with a   2._____
   - A. door
   - B. window
   - C. yard
   - D. bulkhead

3. Of the following, the one which is NOT usually classified as interior wood trim is   3._____
   - A. apron
   - B. ribbon
   - C. jamb
   - D. base mold

4. Single-strength glass would MOST likely be found in   4._____
   - A. single light sash
   - B. doors in fire walls
   - C. doors in fire partitions
   - D. multi-light sash

5. The one of the following items that is LEAST related to the others is   5._____
   - A. newel
   - B. riser
   - C. nosing
   - D. sill

6. Sixteen pieces of 2 x 4 lumber, each 10'6" long, contain a TOTAL of _____ FBM.   6._____
   - A. 110
   - B. 111
   - C. 112
   - D. 113

7. In multiple dwellings, handrails must be provided on each side of a stairway if the stairway exceeds a certain   7._____
   - A. height
   - B. width
   - C. steepness
   - D. tread-riser ratio

8. The base composition of *drywall* is   8._____
   - A. vermiculite
   - B. perlite
   - C. gypsum
   - D. Portland cement

9. The specifications for a construction job state: Furnish and erect chair rail of birch with continuous kerfing where required by room finish schedule.
   Kerfing means MOST NEARLY   9._____
   - A. planing
   - B. rounding
   - C. jointing
   - D. grooving

10. Headers and trimmers are used in the construction of   10._____
    - A. footings
    - B. walls
    - C. floors
    - D. arches

11. In the design of stairs, the designer should consider　　　　　　　　　　11.＿＿＿＿

    A. maximum height of riser *only*
    B. minimum width of tread *only*
    C. product of riser height by tread width *only*
    D. all of the above

12. A reduction in the required number of columns in a building can be made by using one of　　12.＿＿＿＿
    the following types of beam.
    Which one?

    A. Floor　　　　　B. Girder　　　　　C. Cantilever　　　　　D. Jack

13. Doors sheathed in metal are known as ＿＿＿＿＿＿ doors.　　　　　　　13.＿＿＿＿

    A. kalamein　　　　　　　　　　B. tin-clad
    C. bethlehem　　　　　　　　　　D. flemish

14. In the wood frame shown at the right,　　　　　　　　　　　　　　14.＿＿＿＿
    whose corners are all square, the TOTAL
    length of one inch board is ＿＿＿＿＿＿
    inches.
    A. 40
    B. 42
    C. 44
    D. 46

15. Floor beams are sometimes crowned to　　　　　　　　　　　　　　15.＿＿＿＿

    A. provide arch action
    B. eliminate deflection
    C. strengthen the floor
    D. provide a more nearly level floor than would be provided by straight beams

16. Cracks in lumber due to contraction along annual rings are known as　　　　16.＿＿＿＿

    A. checks　　　　　　　　　　B. wanes
    C. pitch pockets　　　　　　　　D. dry rot

17. Of the following, the one which would LEAST likely be used in conjunction with the others　17.＿＿＿＿
    is

    A. rafter　　　　　　　　　　B. collar beam
    C. ridgeboard　　　　　　　　D. tail beam

18. The dimensions of a 2 x 4 when dressed are MOST NEARLY　　　　　　　18.＿＿＿＿

    A. 2" x 4"　　　　　　　　　　B. 1½" x 3½"
    C. 1 5/8" x 3 5/8"　　　　　　D. 1¾" x 3½"

12

19. A piece of wood covering the plaster below the stool of a window is called a(n)   19.____

    A. apron   B. sill   C. coping   D. trimmer

20. The BEST wood to use for handles of tools such as axes and hammers is   20.____

    A. hemlock   B. pine   C. oak   D. hickory

21. Tongue and groove flooring is shown in Sketch No.   21.____

    A. 1
    B. 2
    C. 3
    D. 4

FLOORING

NO.1

NO.2

NO.3

NO.4

Questions 22-25.

DIRECTIONS: Questions 22 through 25 are to be answered on the basis of the label pictured below.

LABEL

BREGSON'S CLEAR GLUE HIGHLY FLAMMABLE A clear quick-drying glue	PRECAUTIONS Use with adequate ventilation
For temporary bonding, apply glue to one surface and join immediately	Close container after use
For permanent bonding, apply glue to both surfaces, permit to dry, and press together	Keep out of reach of children
Use for bonding plastic to plastic, plastic to wood, and wood to wood only	Avoid prolonged breathing of vapors and repeated contact with skin
Will not bond at temperatures below 60°	

22. Assume that you, as a member of a repair crew, have been asked to repair a wood banister in the hallway of a house. Since the heat has been turned off, the hallway is very cold, except for the location where you have to make the repair. Another repair crew worker is working at that same location using a blow torch to solder a pipe in the wall.   22.____

The temperature at that location is about 67°. According to the instruction on the above label, the use of this glue to make the necessary repair is

A. *advisable;* the glue will bond wood to wood
B. *advisable;* the heat from the soldering will cause the glue to dry quickly
C. *inadvisable;* the work area temperature is too low
D. *inadvisable;* the glue is highly flammable

23. According to the instructions on the above label, this glue should NOT be used for which of the following applications? 23.____

    A. Affixing a pine table leg to a walnut table
    B. Repairing leaks around pipe joints
    C. Bonding a plastic knob to a cedar drawer
    D. Attaching a lucite knob to a lucite drawer

24. According to the instructions on the above label, using this glue to bond ceramic tile to a plaster wall by coating both surfaces with glue, letting the glue dry, and then pressing the tile to the plaster wall is 24.____

    A. *advisable;* the glue is quick drying and clear
    B. *advisable;* the glue should be permanently affixed to the one surface of the tile only
    C. *inadvisable;* the glue is not suitable for bonding ceramic tile to plaster walls
    D. *inadvisable;* the bonding should be a temporary one

25. The precaution described in the above label, *Use with adequate ventilation,* means that 25.____

    A. the area you are working in should be very cold
    B. there should be sufficient fresh air where you are using the glue
    C. you should wear gloves to avoid contact with the glue
    D. you must apply a lot of glue to make a permanent bond

KEY (CORRECT ANSWERS)

1. A		11. D
2. B		12. C
3. B		13. A
4. D		14. C
5. D		15. D
6. C		16. A
7. B		17. D
8. C		18. C
9. D		19. A
10. C		20. D

21. A
22. D
23. B
24. C
25. B

TEST 2

DIRECTIONS: Each question or incomplete statement is followed by several suggested answers or completions. Select the one that BEST answers the question or completes the statement. *PRINT THE LETTER OF THE CORRECT ANSWER IN THE SPACE AT THE RIGHT.*

1. A post supporting a handrail is known as a   1.____

    A. tread   B. riser   C. newel   D. bevel

2. The live load on a floor is 40 pounds per square foot. The floor joists are on a 14'0" span and are spaced 2'6" on centers.   2.____
The MAXIMUM live load carried by a joist is, in pounds, MOST NEARLY

    A. 700   B. 933   C. 1167   D. 1400

3. Of the following terms, the one LEAST related to the others is   3.____

    A. ground   B. purlin
    C. rafter   D. ridge board

4. If a hand saw becomes worn so that the teeth are no longer properly set, the   4.____

    A. blade will lose its temper
    B. saw will not cut straight
    C. cut will have jagged edges
    D. blade will tend to bind in the cut

5. Many portable electric power tools, such as electric drills, have a third conductor in the power lead which is used to connect the case of the tool to a grounded part of the electric outlet.   5.____
The reason for this extra conductor is to

    A. have a spare wire in case one power wire should break
    B. strengthen the power lead so it cannot easily be damaged
    C. prevent the user of the tool from being shocked
    D. enable the tool to be used for long periods of time without overheating

6. A non-bearing wall in skeleton construction built between columns and wholly supported at each story is a _____ wall.   6.____

    A. party   B. partition   C. panel   D. fire

7. The part of a window that holds the glass is the   7.____

    A. jamb   B. sash   C. casing   D. bead

8. A one-panel door has two stiles and _____ rails.   8.____

    A. no   B. one   C. two   D. three

9. The vertical part of a stair step is a   9.____

    A. kick-plate   B. tread
    C. landing   D. riser

10. When the joist hanger is used, the joists and girder are fitted together
    A. by notching the joists *only*
    B. by notching the girder *only*
    C. by notching both the joists and the girder
    D. without notching either the joists or girder

10._____

11. Small wood members which are inserted in a diagonal position between floor joists for the purpose of bracing the joists and spreading loads to adjacent joists are called

11._____

    A. struts   B. ties
    C. bridging   D. ledger strips

12. A beam placed perpendicular to joists and to which joists are nailed in framing for a chimney, stairway, or other opening is called a

12._____

    A. trimmer joist   B. tail beam
    C. girder   D. header

13. A narrow board let into the studding to provide added support for joists is known as a

13._____

    A. sill   B. trimmer   C. ribbon   D. sole plate

14. In the city, metal door frames are USUALLY set in place by

14._____

    A. carpenters
    B. structural steel workers
    C. miscellaneous iron workers
    D. masons

15. When inspecting the installation of wood trim, you find that one of the carpenters is leaving the round imprint of his hammer around almost every nail.
    Of the following, the BEST way for you to treat this situation is to

15._____

    A. recommend that this carpenter be removed
    B. recommend that the damaged trim be removed
    C. warn the carpenter that he must be more careful
    D. recommend that the specifications be changed to call for a harder wood

16. A casement window is USUALLY a window that

16._____

    A. is double hung   B. opens inwardly only
    C. is made of wood   D. is pivoted vertically

Questions 17-25.

DIRECTIONS: Questions 17 through 25 are to be answered SOLELY on the basis of the following instructions for carpentry work on elevated stations. Read these instructions carefully before answering these items.

CARPENTRY WORK ON ELEVATED STATIONS

Joists are to be 3 inches by 10 inches and bridging shall be 2 inches by 4 inches. All joists are to be yellow pine, spaced 20 inches on centers. Joists having a span of from 8 feet to 16 feet are to have one row of cross-bridging while spans of over 16 feet are to have two rows of cross-bridging. Bridging shall be nailed at each end. The joists are fastened to the steel supporting beams with special clips. Wood flooring for train platforms is to be yellow pine, 2 inches by 6 inches, dressed four sides, laid transversely with 1/4-inch open joints and is not to be used in lengths of less than five feet. Service walks (track walks) are to consist of five lengths of slatting laid side by side and continuously. The slatting is to be 2 inches by 6 inches and of random lengths varying upward in multiples of four feet six inches. Slatting is to be fastened to each support by two twenty penny cut nails.

17. Joists are fastened to the supporting beams with   17._____

    A. special clips   B. ordinary nails
    C. twenty penny nails   D. screws

18. Slatting may be used without cutting if it has a length of   18._____

    A. 4 feet   B. 4 feet 5 inches
    C. 9 feet   D. 12 feet

19. Joists shall be   19._____

    A. 3" x 5" yellow pine   B. 3" x 10" yellow pine
    C. 3" x 6" spruce   D. 2" x 8" spruce

20. Wood which is dressed four sides is used for   20._____

    A. bridging   B. joists
    C. service walks   D. train platform flooring

21. The center spacing of joists is to be   21._____

    A. 15 inches   B. 20 inches
    C. 5 feet 4 inches   D. 7 feet

22. The number of rows of cross-bridging required for joists having a span of 18 feet is   22._____

    A. four   B. three   C. two   D. one

23. Slatting is fastened   23._____

    A. to every other joist   B. with ten penny nails
    C. to each support   D. with special clips

24. Service walks are to have a width of _____ slats.   24._____

    A. 3   B. 4   C. 5   D. 6

25. Wood which is to be 2" x 6" is for   25._____

    A. platform flooring and the track walks
    B. the bridging *only*
    C. the track walks and the joists
    D. platform flooring and the bridging

KEY (CORRECT ANSWERS)

1.	C	11.	C
2.	D	12.	D
3.	A	13.	C
4.	D	14.	A
5.	C	15.	B
6.	C	16.	D
7.	B	17.	A
8.	C	18.	C
9.	D	19.	B
10.	D	20.	D

21.	B
22.	C
23.	C
24.	C
25.	A

TEST 3

DIRECTIONS: Each question or incomplete statement is followed by several suggested answers or completions. Select the one that BEST answers the question or completes the statement. *PRINT THE LETTER OF THE CORRECT ANSWER IN THE SPACE AT THE RIGHT.*

1. Of the following statements relating to the plies in plywood, the one that is CORRECT is: 1.____

   A. The primary difference between exterior and interior plywood is the quality of the exterior plies
   B. Exterior plywood has more plies than interior plywood
   C. Exterior plywood has no surface defects on the outer plies while interior plywood permits surface defects on the outer plies
   D. Plywood has an odd number of plies

2. Of the following, the one that is NOT a principal classification of lumber according to the American Lumber Standards is   2.____

   A. building   B. structural
   C. yard   D. shop

3. Of the following types of lumber, the one that is classified as a hardwood is   3.____

   A. cedar   B. fir   C. pine   D. maple

Questions 4-6.

DIRECTIONS: Questions 4 through 6 are to be answered SOLELY on the basis of the following passage.

A utility plan is a floor plan which shows the layout of a heating, electrical, plumbing, or other utility system. Utility plans are used primarily by the persons responsible for the utilities, but they are important to the craftsman as well. Most utility installations require the leaving of openings in walls, floors, and roofs for the admission or installation of utility features. The craftsman who is, for example, pouring a concrete foundation wall must study the utility plans to determine the number, sizes, and locations of the openings he must leave for piping, electric lines, and the like.

4. The one of the following items of information which is LEAST likely to be provided by a utility plan is the   4.____

   A. location of the joists and frame members around stairwells
   B. location of the hot water supply and return piping
   C. location of light fixtures
   D. number of openings in the floor for radiators

5. According to the above passage, the persons who will MOST likely have the GREATEST need for the information included in a utility plan of a building are those who   5.____

   A. maintain and repair the heating system
   B. clean the premises
   C. paint housing exteriors
   D. advertise property for sale

19

6. According to the above passage, a repair crew member should find it MOST helpful to consult a utility plan when information is needed about the   6._____

    A. thickness of all doors in the structure
    B. number of electrical outlets located throughout the structure
    C. dimensions of each window in the structure
    D. length of a roof rafter

7. A piece of lumber with a cross-section as shown at the right is called a   7._____

    A. crown moulding   B. panel moulding
    C. shoe moulding   D. quarter round

8. A nut is shown with a wrench placed on it in positions 1 and 2. The numbered arrows show the directions of forces applied to the wrench to turn it. In order to tighten the nut, the CORRECT combination of wrench position and direction of applied force is   8._____

    A. 1-3
    B. 1-4
    C. 2-5
    D. 2-6

9. The upright finished board in the side of a door opening is called a   9._____

    A. batten   B. saddle   C. jamb   D. stile

10. Which one of the following terms is LEAST related to the others?   10._____

    A. Stop   B. Jamb   C. Buck   D. Siding

11. Which one of the following terms is LEAST related to the others?   11._____

    A. Pipe   B. Riser   C. Tread   D. Nosing

12. Of the following terms, the one which is LEAST related to the others is   12._____

    A. baseboard   B. base mold
    C. casing   D. base plate

13. When marking and sawing a timber to a desired length, it is good practice to mark   13._____

    A. slightly smaller than the length and saw just outside the line on the waste side
    B. the exact length and cut just outside the line on the waste side
    C. the exact length and cut on the line
    D. slightly larger than the length and cut on the line

14. If the drawing of a carpentry detail is made to a scale of 3/4" to the foot, a scaled measurement of 6" would represent a length of   14._____

    A. 3/8 inches   B. 8 inches
    C. 4½ feet   D. 8 feet

15. In order to clear the jamb, the lock-edge of a door must be beveled.   15._____
    The bevel must be GREATEST when the door is

    A. wide and thin   B. wide and thick
    C. narrow and thin   D. narrow and thick

16. The saw shown at the right would be   16._____
    used to cut
    A. curved designs in thin wood
    B. strap iron
    C. asphalt tiles to fit against walls
    D. soft lead pipe

17. The timbers that support the rough flooring are called   17._____

    A. lintels   B. sills   C. beams   D. studs

18. Wood for the wearing surface of a floor should PREFERABLY be   18._____

    A. flat-sawed   B. quarter-sawed
    C. cross-cut   D. rip-sawed

19. Wainscoting is   19._____

    A. the moulding around a room for hanging pictures
    B. the moulding around a room to protect the plaster from the backs of chairs
    C. panel work covering part or all of a wall
    D. the tile or cement flooring in a kitchen around the stove or range

20. Of the following, the one that is NOT a defect of lumber is   20._____

    A. wane   B. plinth   C. check   D. shake

21. A specification reads: Douglas fir shall average on either one end or the other not less   21._____
    than 6 nor more than 20 annual rings per inch over a 3-inch portion of a radial line.
    The object of this requirement is to secure lumber that is

    A. of beautiful grain   B. close-grained
    C. free of knots   D. chiefly heartwood

22. Of the following grades of lumber, the BEST grade is   22._____

    A. No. 1 Common   B. No. 2 Common
    C. Select Grade A   D. Select Grade B

23. Twist drills ranging in size from 5/16" to 1/2" and having 1/4" shanks are available for use   23._____
    in electric drills. These drills are designed in this manner so that they may be used

    A. in $\frac{1}{4}$" electric drills for high speed drilling of steel

    B. in $\frac{1}{4}$" electric drills for drilling wood

    C. when it is important that, if the twist drill breaks, it does not do so in the hole being
       drilled

    D. in $\frac{1}{2}$" electric drills in order to increase the peripheral speed of the twist drill

24. The wrench is shown in position to unloosen a tight nut. If the hand is placed on the wrench at A, the force necessary to start the nut as compared to the force necessary if the hand were placed at B would be

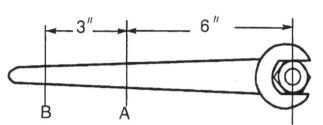

    A. 150%
    B. 110%
    C. 85%
    D. 70%

24._____

25. The tool that should be used to cut a 1" x 4" plank down to a 3" width is a

    A. hacksaw   B. crosscut saw
    C. rip saw   D. backsaw

25._____

KEY (CORRECT ANSWERS)

1.	D		11.	A
2.	A		12.	D
3.	D		13.	B
4.	A		14.	D
5.	A		15.	D
6.	B		16.	A
7.	D		17.	C
8.	D		18.	B
9.	C		19.	C
10.	D		20.	B

21.	B
22.	C
23.	B
24.	A
25.	C

CARPENTRY

EXAMINATION SECTION
TEST 1

DIRECTIONS: Each question or incomplete statement is followed by several suggested answers or completions. Select the one that BEST answers the question or completes the statement. *PRINT THE LETTER OF THE CORRECT ANSWER IN THE SPACE AT THE RIGHT.*

1. In a ratchet bit brace, the part that holds the bit is called the   1.____

   A. vise   B. chuck   C. pawl   D. cam ring

2. The BEST tool to use as a guide when scribing a line perpendicular to the side of a 2" x 4" stud is a   2.____

   A. T-square   B. Try square
   C. Batter board   D. Parallel bar

3. Of the following planes, the *one* that does NOT have a double plane iron is the   3.____

   A. block plane   B. jack plane
   C. fore plane   D. smooth plane

4. Of the following files, the BEST one to use to sharpen a rip-saw is a   4.____

   A. taper   B. flat bastard   C. mill   D. half round

5. The size of auger bit to select in order to bore a 5/8" hole is   5.____

   A. #5   B. #8   C. #10   D. #12

6. The type of circular saw used for cutting grooves that are *wider* than the cut that can be made by ordinary saws is known as a   6.____

   A. dado set   B. rabbet set
   C. scarf set   D. dove tail set

7. Of the following saws, the *one* that should be used for cutting circular disks out of 5/8" plywood is a   7.____

   A. circular saw   B. buck saw
   C. back saw   D. band saw

8. The saw used in a miter box is a   8.____

   A. compass saw   B. coping saw
   C. back saw   D. hacksaw

9. Of the following, the BEST wood to use for the handle of a claw hammer is   9.____

   A. pine   B. hickory   C. cypress   D. elm

10. A 3" belt sander requires a 3 x 21 belt. The "21" refers to the belt's   10.____

    A. grit number   B. diameter
    C. contact area   D. length

11. In sharpening a paring chisel, a carpenter should grind the bevel at an angle of, *approxi-*   11.____
mately,

     A.   5°   B.   15°   C.   25°   D.   35°

12. "Dressing" a saw has to do with   12.____

     A.   lowering the height of the teeth
     B.   removing burrs from the side of the teeth
     C.   lowering of the tooth gullets
     D.   tilting the file upward at the end of the stroke

13. To cut a 1/4-inch chamfer in a piece of wood two feet long, a carpenter should use a   13.____

     A.   chisel   B.   plane   C.   saw   D.   hone

14. To tighten a lag screw, a Carpenter should use a   14.____

     A.   mallet   B.   Phillips head screw-driver
     C.   wrench   D.   hammer

15. When boring a hole through a thin piece of wood, the bit that will LEAST splinter the   15.____
backside of the wood is a(n)

     A.   center bit   B.   expensive bit
     C.   Foerstner bit   D.   countersink bit

16. Shown below is a sketch of a hinge.   16.____

The hinge is a(n)

     A.   T-hinge   B.   strap hinge
     C.   piano hinge   D.   offset hinge

17. A hinged strap with a slotted flap that passes over a staple and is secured by a padlock is   17.____
known as a

     A.   hasp   B.   hamper   C.   harbinger   D.   hawk

18. To bend saw teeth to the proper angle, a carpenter should use a   18.____

     A.   saw screed   B.   saw tap   C.   saw bit   D.   saw set

19. A tool used to make a pilot hole for starting a screw in wood is a(n)   19.____

     A.   grommet   B.   cotter pin   C.   awl   D.   counter point

20. The tool to use to finish driving a nail into corners and moldings is a nail   20.____

     A.   set   B.   punch   C.   pin   D.   all

21. Of the following fasteners, the *one* that is LEAST often used in structural wood work is a   21.____

    A. lag screw   B. wood screw   C. nail   D. spike

22. When wood loses moisture, it shrinks in   22.____

    A. thickness and width and expands in length
    B. thickness and expands in width and length
    C. width and length and expands in thickness
    D. thickness, width, and length

23. Of the following types of commercial nails, the *one* that has the GREATEST withdrawal resistance is a   23.____

    A. cement-coated nail   B. galvanized nail
    C. chemically etched nail   D. spirally grooved nail

24. The grit number for a 1/0 sand paper is   24.____

    A. 200   B. 100   C. 80   D. 60

25. The length of a 6d nail is   25.____

    A. 1 3/4"   B. 2"   C. 2 1/4"   D. 2 3/4"

KEYS (CORRECT ANSWERS)

1.	B		11.	B
2.	B		12.	B
3.	A		13.	B
4.	A		14.	C
5.	C		15.	A
6.	A		16.	D
7.	D		17.	A
8.	C		18.	D
9.	B		19.	C
10.	D		20.	A

21.	B
22.	D
23.	D
24.	C
25.	B

TEST 2

Each question or incomplete statement is followed by several suggested answers or completions. Select the one that BEST answers the question or completes the statement. *PRINT THE LETTER OF THE CORRECT ANSWER IN THE SPACE AT THE RIGHT.*

1. The number of board feet in 15 pieces of lumber 2" x 10" by 12 feet long is   1.____

   A. 30   B. 300   C. 600   D. 900

2. When unpainted wood is left outdoors for a considerable time, the color of the wood *usually* changes to   2.____

   A. brown   B. gray   C. yellow   D. amber

3. When wood is to be in permanent contact with earth, it should be treated with   3.____

   A. creosote   B. tri-sodium phosphate
   C. sodium chloride   D. sal ammoniac

4. A panic bolt is *most frequently* installed on a   4.____

   A. window   B. door   C. roof scuttle   D. skylight

5. Of the following, the BEST reason for oiling plywood concrete forms is to   5.____

   A. lubricate the concrete during vibration
   B. allow forms to be removed easily
   C. decrease porosity of the plywood
   D. prevent seapage of rain water into the concrete in case it rains while the concrete is setting

6. Of the following species of wood, the *one* that is classified as a SOFT wood is   6.____

   A. chestnut   B. white ash   C. birch   D. cypress

7. S.S. glass means   7.____

   A. Smooth Surface glass   B. Silicone Surface glass
   C. Single Strength glass   D. Square Sides glass

8. Of the following types of wood, the *one* that is NOT coarsegrained is   8.____

   A. oak   B. pine   C. walnut   D. chestnut

9. The one of the following materials that does NOT contain wood is   9.____

   A. hardboard   B. compressed board
   C. particle board   D. masonite

10. Plywood sub flooring is used instead of 1" x 6" sub flooring MAINLY because it   10.____

   A. is more sound proof   B. is easier to install
   C. is more fire resistant   D. makes the floor more rigid

11. Wainscoting paneling would be installed on a   11.____

   A. wall   B. floor   C. ceiling   D. roof

12. According to the building code, galvanized wire staple fasteners in plywood may   12.____

    A. not be used anywhere in buildings
    B. be used on roofs only
    C. be used on wall sheathing only
    D. be used on roofs and wall sheathing

13. Galvanized nails are nails that are coated with   13.____

    A. brass   B. cadmium   C. copper   D. zinc

14. The tip of a Phillips screwdriver is   14.____

    A. elliptical   B. pointed   C. flat   D. concave

15. Putlogs are used PRIMARILY on   15.____

    A. ladders   B. scaffolds   C. horses   D. hatchways

16. The tapered end of a file that fits into a wood handle is called the   16.____

    A. tip   B. heel   C. edge   D. tang

17. Of the following bolts, the type which has a *round* head is the   17.____

    A. machine bolt   B. stud bolt
    C. carriage bolt   D. coupling bolt

18. A metal T-anchor would be used on a   18.____

    A. door   B. window   C. joist   D. stud

19. A lock that is surface mounted on the side of a door is known as a   19.____

    A. rim lock   B. tenon lock
    C. mortise lock   D. flange lock

20. Clapboards are *generally* used for   20.____

    A. stair treads   B. wood siding
    C. window sills   D. roof copings

21. Shown below is a sketch of the floor joists in a building.   21.____

FLOOR JOIST

ELEVATION

The pieces of wood marked X are known as

    A. bridging   B. bracketing   C. corbeling   D. casing

22. A specification for a belt sander states that it is *UL* approved. The *UL* in the specification is an abbreviation of

    A. Universal Listing   B. Underwriters Laboratories
    C. Unlimited Liability   D. Use Limited

22.____

23. Shown below is a sketch of a wood joint.

23.____

PLAN

ELEVATION

The wood joint is a

    A. peg tenon   B. plain dovetail butt
    C. dovetail half lap   D. blind housed tenon

Questions 24-25.

DIRECTIONS: Questions 24 and 25 refer to the wood form work for concrete shown in the sketch at the top of the next page.

24. The horizontal member X is known as a

    A. girt   B. soldier   C. pivot   D. waler

24.____

25. The horizontal member Y is known as a

    A. scab   B. ledger   C. kerf   D. putlog

25.____

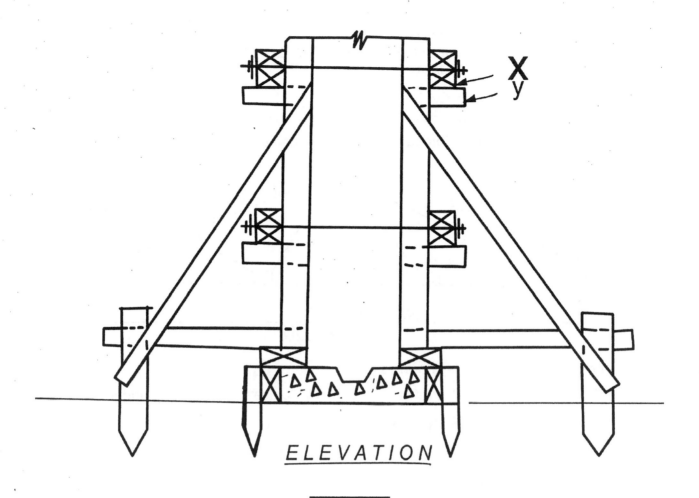

X
y

ELEVATION

KEYS (CORRECT ANSWERS)

1.	B		11.	A
2.	B		12.	D
3.	A		13.	D
4.	B		14.	B
5.	B		15.	B
6.	D		16.	D
7.	C		17.	C
8.	B		18.	C
9.	B		19.	A
10.	B		20.	B

21.	A
22.	B
23.	A
24.	D
25.	B

TEST 3

DIRECTIONS: Each question or incomplete statement is followed by several suggested answers or completions. Select the one that BEST answers the question or completes the statement. *PRINT THE LETTER OF THE CORRECT ANSWER IN THE SPACE AT THE RIGHT.*

Questions 1-3.

DIRECTIONS: Questions 1 through 3 refer to the wood truss shown in the sketch below.

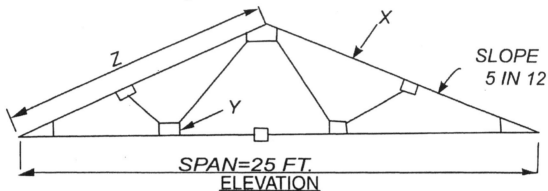

1. The inclined member X is known as a   1.____

    A. ridge   B. rafter   C. brace   D. bridge

2. The plate marked Y is known as a(n)   2.____

    A. gusset   B. batten   C. spacer   D. anchor

3. The TOTAL distance Z is, *most nearly,*   3.____

    A. 13' 2 1/2"   B. 13' 4 1/2"
    C. 13' 6 1/2"   D. 13' 8 1/2"

4. Shown in the sketch below is a bolted timber.   4.____

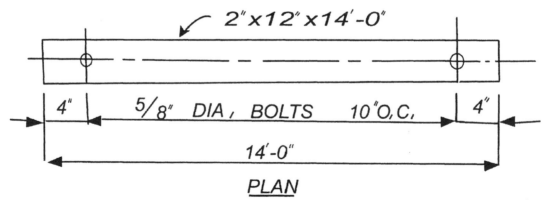

The number of 5/8" diameter bolts required is

    A. 15   B. 16   C. 17   D. 18

5. Plywood sub flooring 5/8" thick has a Panel Identification Index of 42/20. The "20" indicates the

    A. maximum allowable load in pounds on a square foot of panel
    B. maximum permitted center to center distance in inches between floor joists
    C. weight of a cubic foot of panel
    D. minimum number of 8d nails required per panel

    5.____

6. An identifying symbol *HDO* G-1 - DFPA - 19 - PS1 - 66 is stamped on the edge of a plywood panel. The *HDO* part of this code stands for

    A. Heavy Duty Outside
    B. High Density Oak
    C. High Density Overlaid
    D. Housing Development Organization

    6.____

7. Floor plans showing the modification of partitions are drawn to a scale of 1/4" to a foot. If the length of a partition shown on the drawing scales 6 3/8", then the ACTUAL length of the partition would be, *most nearly,*

    A. 2.4' 6"   B. 25' 2"   C. 24' 4"   D. 25' 6"

    7.____

Questions 8-9.

DIRECTIONS: Questions 8 and 9 refer to the DETAIL shown below.

ROOF SCUTTLE DETAIL

8. The number of 3/8" bolts in the roof scuttle is

    A. 6   B. 8   C. 10   D. 12

    8.____

9. In the DETAIL shown above, the number of 2" x 6" planks required is

    A. 7   B. 8   C. 9   D. 10

    9.____

10. On an alteration drawing, the location of *new* partitions would be shown on a(n)

    A. floor plan   B. front elevation
    C. frame cross-section   D. end view

    10.____

11. A drawing specifies "3-1x6-*Fas* - Wh. Oak S4S." *Fas* is an abbreviation for

    A. face all sides   B. finish all sides
    C. fabricate as specified   D. firsts and seconds

    11.____

12.   12.____

In the trade mark shown above, the abbreviation DFPA means

    A.   Designers Fabricated Partition Authority
    B.   Douglas Fir Plywood Association
    C.   Developed Fabricated Plyscord Association
    D.   Durable Federal Product Authority

13. A specification calls for *3/8" x 2"* steel lag screw. In the above specification, the *3/8"* refers   13.____
to the

    A.   height of the head
    B.   root diameter of the thread
    C.   diameter of the body under the head
    D.   length of body under the head

14. The following statement is taken from a specification scope of work: 14.____
    Except as otherwise specified, furnish, deliver and install all carpentry and millwork,
related work and equipment as required by the drawings and specified herein, including, but not necessarily limited to the following:
    All rough carpentry work where shown on the drawings, implied as necessary,
specified, or otherwise required including permanent and temporary grounds, blocking,
rough framing and *bucks,* nailing strips, furring, plates, under floor sleepers, and the
like.
In the above passage, *bucks* would refer to

    A.   doors   B.   windows   C.   scuppers   D.   hatchways

15. A specification states the floowing: 15.____
    Blind nail T and G flooring.
In the above specification, the word *blind* means to

    A.   bend   B.   hide   C.   extrude   D.   offset

16. Narrow strips of wood nailed upon walls and ceilings as a support for the wall or ceiling   16.____
finish is known as

    A.   darbying   B.   batting   C.   heading   D.   furring

17. A purlin is *most similar* in function to a   17.____

    A.   stud   B.   jamb   C.   joist   D.   batten

18. If the riser for a stairway is 7 1/2" high, then the *number* of risers required for a flight of   18.____
stairs 8' 9" high is

    A.   11   B.   12   C.   13   D.   14

19. The one of the following that is NOT a common type of wood joint is the   19._____

    A. scarf   B. dovetail   C. chamfer   D. butt

20. A flat hardwood board set on the floor in a doorway between rooms is called a   20._____

    A. mullion   B. jamb   C. jib   D. saddle

21. Shown below is a section of wall and flooring of a building.   21._____

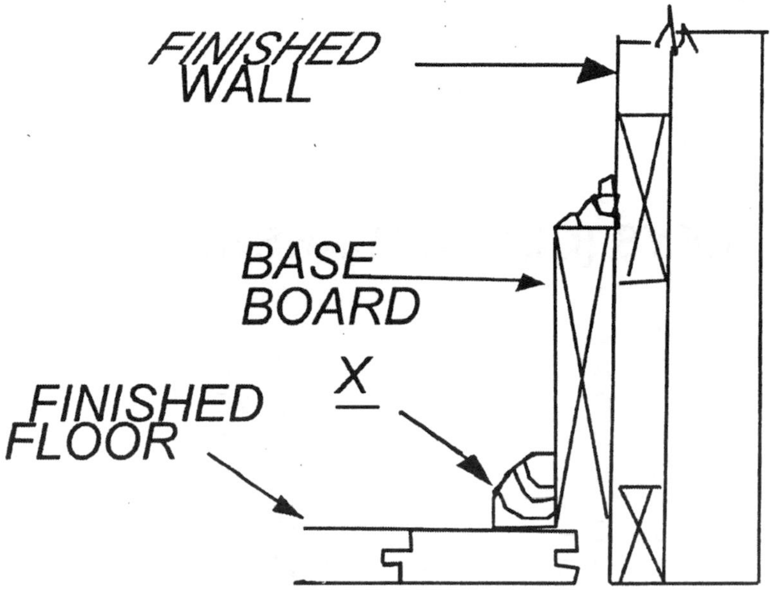

In the drawing shown above, the molding X represents a

    A. base mold   B. shoe mold   C. bed mold   D. lip mold

22. Shown below is a section through a door.   22._____

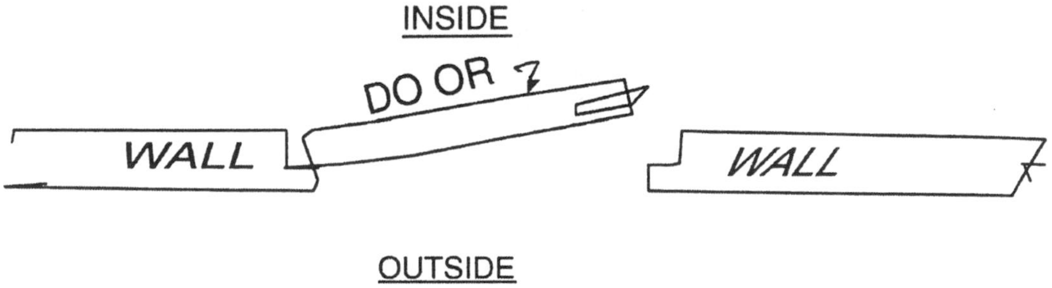

The hand of the door is

    A. left hand regular   B. left hand reverse
    C. right hand regular   D. right hand reverse

23. A 3/4" thick flooring is to be laid directly on joists.   23._____
    Of the following, the BEST practice is to nail the flooring to

    A. every joist
    B. every third joist
    C. end joists only
    D. end joists and middle joist only

24. The margin which should be left all around between the edges of an 8" x 10" pane of glass and the sides of the rabbet in a wood sash is   24.____

    A. none   B. 1/16"   C. 3/16"   D. 5/16"

25. The *horizontal* wood member which supports the load over a window or door is known as a   25.____

    A. putlog   B. ledger   C. collar   D. lintel

KEYS (CORRECT ANSWERS)

1.	B		11.	D
2.	A		12.	B
3.	C		13.	C
4.	C		14.	A
5.	B		15.	B
6.	C		16.	D
7.	D		17.	C
8.	D		18.	D
9.	D		19.	C
10.	A		20.	D

21.	B
22.	A
23.	A
24.	B
25.	D

TEST 4

DIRECTIONS: Each question or incomplete statement is followed by several suggested answers or completions. Select the one that BEST answers the question or completes the statement. *PRINT THE LETTER OF THE CORRECT ANSWER IN THE SPACE AT THE RIGHT.*

1. Shown below is a section of a wood joint.

1.____

ELEVATION

The joint shown is a

   A. dove tail joint   B. double butt joint
   C. shiplap joint   D. serrated joint

2. In the construction of a wood frame building a metal shield is sometimes placed between the top of concrete piers and the wood girder resting on it. Of the following, the BEST reason for the metal shield is to

2.____

   A. spread the load over the pier
   B. protect the wood against termites
   C. insulate the building
   D. allow for expansion and contraction of the wood

3. Shown below is a section of wood molding.

3.____

The molding is a(n)

   A. reed   B. center bead   C. round   D. astragal

4. Wood is *most frequently* fastened to a concrete wall by a(n)

4.____

   A. clevis   B. expansion shield
   C. brad   D. spike

5. A bolt with a spring loaded part used for securing wood to a hollow wall is a(n)

5.____

   A. anchor bolt   B. stud bolt
   C. toggle bolt   D. toe bolt

6. The *number* of plane surfaces in a gambrel roof is

6.____

   A. two   B. three   C. four   D. five

7. The *vertical* members of a wooden door are known as   7.____

     A.   rails   B.   stiles   C.   struts   D.   sleepers

8. Driving nails at an angle to the surface of a vertical member in order to get adequate   8.____
penetration into a horizontal member is known as

     A.   clinch nailing   B.   toe nailing
     C.   French nailing   D.   dog nailing

9. Collar beams are *most often* used on   9.____

     A.   trusses   B.   windows   C.   girders   D.   doors

10. On a double-hung wood window, the stool rests on the sill *and* a(n)   10.____

     A.   mullion   B.   rail   C.   apron   D.   stud

11. In a two-story wood frame building, a fascia would be found on the   11.____

     A.   roof   B.   stair   C.   wall   D.   floor

12. A baluster is a part of a   12.____

     A.   roof   B.   wall   C.   door   D.   stair

13. Stair treads rest on strips of wood nailed to the inside of stair stringers. These strips of   13.____
wood are called

     A.   shims   B.   wedges   C.   stubs   D.   cleats

14. Shown at the top of the next page is a section through the exterior wall of a building.   14.____
The member X represents a

     A.   wall plate   B.   ledger
     C.   fire stop   D.   girder

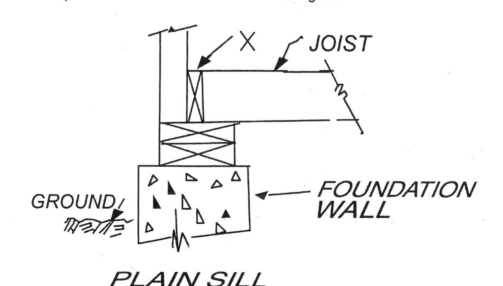

15. The molded projection which finishes the top of the wall of a building is a   15._____

    A. coronet   B. corolla   C. cornice   D. cupola

16. The BEST reason for *not* painting a wood ladder is that   16._____

    A. the paint may conceal cracks
    B. it saves money not to paint the ladder
    C. painted ladder rungs get very slippery when wet
    D. the wood used is difficult to paint and paint spalls readily

17. In case of a fire in the floor below in a building in which a carpenter is making alterations,   17._____
the BEST action for the carpenter to take is to

    A. walk quickly to the nearest stairway
    B. walk quickly to the nearest elevator
    C. collect all his tools and run to the nearest stairway
    D. open all the windows and run to the nearest stairway

18. Of the following, the one that should NOT be used as an improvised tourniquet is a   18._____

    A. leather belt   B. Venetian blind cord
    C. stocking   D. scarf

19. Of the following character traits, the BEST trait for a supervisor to have is   19._____

    A. optimism   B. rudeness   C. punctuality   D. decisiveness

20. Assume that you are acting in charge of a group of carpenters in the field installing parti-   20._____
tions. You receive a telephone call from the office that they need a carpenter in the shop
to do a rush job.
Of the following, the BEST action to take is to

    A. send the senior carpenter
    B. send the most capable carpenter
    C. ask for volunteers
    D. send the least capable carpenter

21. In assigning additional work to carpenters, a supervisor should FIRST consider the car-   21._____
penter's

    A. seniority   B. previous output
    C. current work load   D. attendance record

22. In checking the daily work of several carpenters at different locations, a good supervisor   22._____
should visit the men

    A. according to each man's seniority
    B. at random hours each day
    C. according to location of nearest man first and farthest man last
    D. according to priority of when jobs have to be completed

23. Of the following jobs, the *one* that usually requires WRITTEN orders instead of ORAL orders is a job where   23.____

    A. progress can be easily checked
    B. emergency exists
    C. a mistake will be of little consequence
    D. many details are involved

24. To obtain cooperation from subordinates, a supervisor should   24.____

    A. complain about it   B. practice it
    C. demand it   D. suggest it

25. The BEST way to *temporarily* store oily sawdust in a carpenter shop before discarding the sawdust is in a   25.____

    A. metal can with a perforated metal cover
    B. metal can without a cover
    C. metal can with an air-tight metal cover
    D. perforated metal can with an air-tight cover

KEYS (CORRECT ANSWERS)

1.	C		11.	A
2.	B		12.	D
3.	D		13.	D
4.	B		14.	C
5.	C		15.	C
6.	C		16.	A
7.	B		17.	A
8.	B		18.	B
9.	A		19.	D
10.	C		20.	B

21.	C
22.	B
23.	D
24.	B
25.	C

TEST 5

DIRECTIONS: For questions 1 through 11, the item referred to is shown to the right of the question.

1. The bolt shown should be used
   A. in foundations
   B. in cement curbs
   C. to connect rails
   D. to connect girders

   1.____

2. The screw shown is called a
   A. set screw
   B. anchor screw
   C. lag screw
   D. toggle screw

   2.____

3. The anchor shown should be used in a
   A. wood post
   B. concrete wall
   C. plaster wall
   D. gypsum block wall

   3.____

4. The wrench shown is called a(n)
   A. monkey wrench
   B. Allen wrench
   C. "L" wrench
   D. socket wrench

   4.____

5. The anchor shown should be used in a
   A. concrete wall
   B. veneer wall
   C. plaster wall
   D. brick wall

   5.____

6. The cutter shown should be used on
   A. pipes
   B. cables
   C. re-bars
   D. bolts

   6.____

7. The saw shown is called a
   A. coping saw
   B. cross-cut saw
   C. hack saw
   D. back saw

   7.____

8. The tool shown is a
   A. "D" clamp
   B. "C" clamp
   C. pipe vise
   D. metal vise

   8.____

39

9. The tool shown is a
   A. hawk
   B. trowel
   C. screed
   D. joiner

9.____

10. The tool shown is called a
    A. try square
    B. T-bevel
    C. miter box
    D. miter square

10.____

11. The tool shown should be used to
    A. make grooves in side walks
    B. turn lead bends
    C. make copper bends
    D. finish brick joints

11.____

KEYS (CORRECT ANSWERS)

1.	A		6.	A
2.	C		7.	D
3.	B		8.	B
4.	B		9.	B
5.	C		10.	C
			11.	A

EXAMINATION SECTION
TEST 1

DIRECTIONS: Each question or incomplete statement is followed by several suggested answers or completions. Select the one that BEST answers the question or completes the statement. *PRINT THE LETTER OF THE CORRECT ANSWER IN THE SPACE AT THE RIGHT.*

1. The tool MOST frequently used to lay out a 45° angle on a piece of lumber is a   1.____

    A. combination square   B. try square
    C. marking gauge   D. divider

2. Beeswax would be MOST FREQUENTLY used on a(n)   2.____

    A. auger bit   B. scraper   C. hand saw   D. draw knife

3. A tool used to plane concave edges of furniture is a   3.____

    A. rabbet plane   B. wood scraper
    C. utility knife   D. spoke saw

4. A cap is found on a   4.____

    A. hammer   B. plane   C. power saw   D. lathe

5. The one of the following types of saw blades that is NOT commonly used on a circular saw is a   5.____

    A. dado   B. ply-tooth   C. novelty   D. tyler

6. The diameter of the arbor of a 12" circular saw is MOST LIKELY to be   6.____

    A. 3/8"   B. 1/2"   C. 5/8"   D. 3/4"

7. The one of the following woodworking operations that is NOT easily done on a drill press is   7.____

    A. routing   B. turning   C. shaping   D. mortising

8. A jointer may ALSO be used for   8.____

    A. mortising   B. routing   C. planing   D. shaping

9. The one of the following power tools that is NOT frequently built with a slot for a miter guage is a   9.____

    A. shaper   B. band saw   C. disc sander   D. radial saw

10. The abrasive grit on *sandpaper* is USUALLY   10.____

    A. pumice   B. boron   C. flint   D. talc

11. The abrasive grit on *open coat* paper for use on a power sander for woodwork is USU-ALLY   11.____

    A. tripoli   B. emery   C. aluminum oxide   D. carborundum

12. The one of the following used in finishing furniture that has the FINEST grit is   12.____

    A. garnet   B. carborundum
    C. pumice   D. rottenstone

13. An expansive bit should be sharpened with a(n)   13.____

    A. auger bit file   B. mill file
    C. half round file   D. grinding wheel

14. The one of the following planes that is USUALLY used with one hand is the   14.____

    A. smoothing   B. block   C. jack   D. fore

15. When sharpening a hand saw, the FIRST operation is to file the teeth so that they are all the same height.
This is known as   15.____

    A. shaping   B. setting   C. jointing   D. leveling

16. The tool that would be used to cut out a circular disc is a   16.____

    A. circular saw   B. shaper
    C. planer   D. band saw

17. A scale on which the inch graduations are divided into 12 subdivisions, each 1/12 of an inch in length, is USUALLY found on a _____ square.   17.____

    A. try   B. combination
    C. rafter   D. T

18. The one of the following oils that is COMMONLY used for oilstones is   18.____

    A. penetrating   B. SAE #5
    C. vinsol   D. pike

19. A tool used in hanging doors is a   19.____

    A. butt gauge   B. reamer   C. C-clamp   D. trammel

20. A spur center is used on a   20.____

    A. jigsaw   B. drill press
    C. lathe   D. disc sander

21. The length of a certain screw is measured from the top of the head to the point. The type of screw that this is MOST LIKELY to be is a   21.____

    A. round head   B. flat head   C. oval head   D. lag

22. The size of the drill that would be used to drill a body hole for a #7 wood screw is   22.____

    A. 3/32"   B. 5/32"   C. 7/32"   D. 9/32"

23. The one of the following types of bolts that would be used to anchor a shelf bracket to a plywood partition is a   23.____

    A. carriage   B. expansion   C. drift   D. toggle

24. For ease in driving, screws are FREQUENTLY coated with   24.____

   A. casco   B. oil   C. soap   D. urea resins

25. The length of a 10-penny nail is   25.____

   A. 3"   B. 3 1/4"   C. 3 1/2"   D. 3 3/4"

26. To increase the holding power of nails, the nails are FREQUENTLY coated with   26.____

   A. alundum   B. aluminum   C. zinc   D. cement

27. Galvanized nails would MOST PROBABLY be used in nailing   27.____

   A. shingles   B. finished flooring
   C. joists   D. interior trim

28. Splitting of wood can be reduced by using nails with points that are   28.____

   A. long and sharp   B. blunt
   C. spirally grooved   D. common

29. The standard size of a 2" X 6" S4S is   29.____

   A. 1 5/8" X 5 5/8"   B. 1 5/8" X 5 3/4"
   C. 1 1/2" X 5 1/2"   D. 1 1/2" X 5 5/8"

30. The West Coast Lumber Inspection Bureau has recently changed the names of the   30.____
grades of lumber for Douglas Fir and Hemlock.
The grade that was PREVIOUSLY called No. 1 common is NOW called

   A. construction   B. utility
   C. select   D. structural

31. The strength of lumber is affected by   31.____

   A. whether it is cut from a live tree or a dead tree
   B. the time of the year in which the lumber is cut
   C. whether the tree is virgin growth or second growth
   D. the moisture content of the lumber

32. The one of the following woods that is classed as *open grained* is   32.____

   A. douglas fir   B. long leaf yellow pine
   C. spruce   D. oak

33. The one of the following woods that is classed as a hardwood is   33.____

   A. cedar   B. poplar
   C. douglas fir   D. hemlock

34. The one of the following woods that is MOST difficult to work with hand tools is   34.____

   A. cedar, northern white   B. pine, southern yellow
   C. hemlock, western   D. cypress, southern

35. The one of the following heartwoods that has the GREATEST resistance to decay is   35.____

   A. douglas fir   B. spruce   C. oak   D. birch

36. The one of the following woods that is EASIEST to glue is   36._____

    A. beech   B. birch   C. cedar   D. walnut

37. Flooring, for surfaces that will have very heavy wear, such as gymnasiums, is USUALLY   37._____
    made of

    A. oak   B. maple
    C. long leaf yellow pine   D. larch

38. The BEST grades of finished flooring are _____ sawed.   38._____

    A. quarter   B. flat   C. end   D. plain

39. Lumber used for floor joists in the East is USUALLY   39._____

    A. oak   B. gum   C. hemlock   D. pine

40. The wood MOST COMMONLY used for shingles is   40._____

    A. alder   B. larch   C. cedar   D. spruce

41. Millwork is USUALLY made of   41._____

    A. ash   B. chestnut   C. hemlock   D. pine

42. The wood MOST FREQUENTLY used for the rungs of the BEST quality ladders is   42._____

    A. locust   B. hickory   C. oak   D. balsam

43. Dressed and matched lumber would MOST LIKELY be   43._____

    A. dove-tailed   B. bevel siding
    C. crown molding   D. tongue and groove

44. Creosote is used to   44._____

    A. intensify the grain of wood prior to finishing
    B. preserve wood from rot
    C. glue wood in laminated girders
    D. prevent checking

45. The one of the following that is COMMONLY used as a vapor barrier is   45._____

    A. asphalt roll roofing   B. Kraft paper
    C. plywood   D. gypsum board

46. Corners of a building are USUALLY located by means of   46._____

    A. batter boards   B. framing squares
    C. line levels   D. base plates

47. Horizontal beams used to reinforce concrete forms and sheet piling are known as   47._____

    A. stirrups   B. walers   C. sheathing   D. braces

48. When using a post to shore a form for a reinforced concrete girder, the BEST practice is to cut the post   48._____
    A. to exact length, so that no driving will be required
    B. slightly larger than required, so that the post must be driven into place
    C. with a slight bevel, so that the post can be wedged into place
    D. several inches too short, so that wedges will be needed

49. Corner posts of a frame building in the East MUST be at least the equivalent of three _____ inch timbers.   49._____
    A. 2X4   B. 2X6   C. 3X6   D. 4X4

50. The size of cross bridging between joists is MOST FREQUENTLY   50._____
    A. 1" X 2"   B. 1" X 3"   C. 2" X 4"   D. 2" X 6"

KEY (CORRECT ANSWERS)

1. A	11. C	21. B	31. D	41. D
2. C	12. D	22. B	32. D	42. B
3. D	13. A	23. D	33. B	43. D
4. B	14. B	24. C	34. B	44. B
5. D	15. C	25. A	35. A	45. A
6. D	16. D	26. D	36. C	46. A
7. B	17. C	27. A	37. B	47. B
8. C	18. D	28. B	38. A	48. D
9. D	19. A	29. A	39. C	49. A
10. C	20. C	30. A	40. C	50. B

TEST 2

DIRECTIONS: Each question or incomplete statement is followed by several suggested answers or completions. Select the one that BEST answers the question or completes the statement. *PRINT THE LETTER OF THE CORRECT ANSWER IN THE SPACE AT THE RIGHT.*

1. The MAXIMUM spacing between bridging should be   1.____

   A. 6 ft.   B. 8 ft.   C. 10 ft.   D. 12 ft.

2. The one of the following methods of nailing cross bridging that is the MOST ACCEPT-ABLE is   2.____

   A. the tops and bottoms should be nailed before the subflooring is in place
   B. the tops and bottoms should be nailed after the subflooring is in place
   C. *only* the bottoms should be nailed. The tops should be nailed after the subflooring is in place
   D. *only* the tops should be nailed. The bottoms should be nailed after the subflooring is in place

3. The one of the following that may be used as a shim to raise the end of a joist resting on a concrete wall is   3.____

   A. gypsum block   B. wood
   C. sheet rock   D. slate

4. When framing joists around a chimney, the MINIMUM clear distance from wood to the chimney permitted in the East is   4.____

   A. 4"   B. 6"   C. 8"   D. 10"

5. The ends of joists are FREQUENTLY supported on   5.____

   A. hanger bolts   B. tie plates
   C. bridle irons   D. gusset plates

6. When there is a tight knot in a joist, the joist should   6.____

   A. be placed with the knot up
   B. be placed with the knot down
   C. be reinforced
   D. not be used

7.

7.____

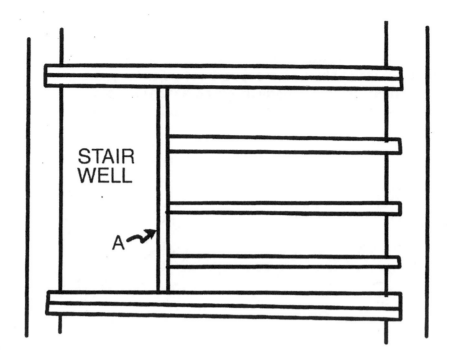

The short joist indicated by the letter *A* above is known as

A.   trimmer   B.   tail beam   C.   header   D.   lattice

8.

8.____

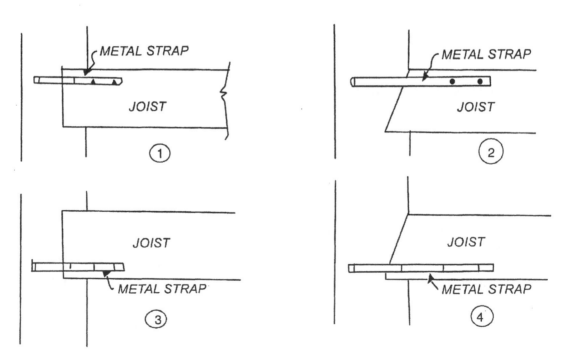

The diagram above that shows the BEST method of anchoring a wood joist to a brick is numbered

A.   *1*   B.   *2*   C.   *3*   D.   *4*

9. Where a non bearing partition runs over and is parallel to the joists, standard practice requires that   9._____

    A. a post be placed midway under the joist supporting the partition
    B. sag rods be used to transfer the load to the adjoining joists
    C. the joist directly under the partition be increased in depth
    D. the joist directly under the partition be doubled

10.   10._____

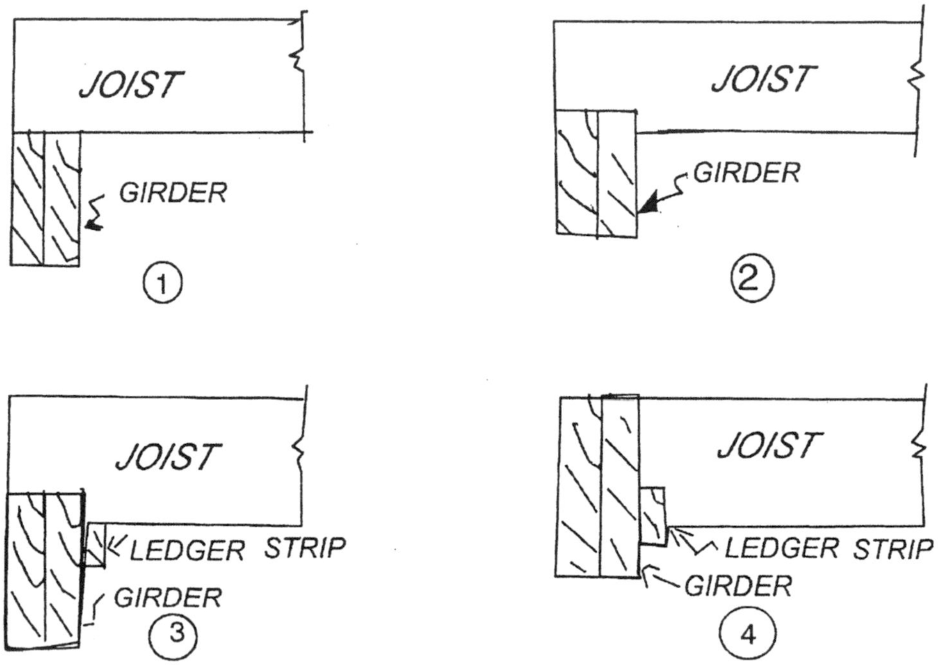

The diagram above that shows the BEST method of supporting a joist on a girder is numbered

    A. 1   B. 2   C. 3   D. 4

11. The one of the following statements that is CORRECT when *roofers* are used for sub-flooring is diagonal subflooring   11._____

    A. requires less lumber than subflooring applied at right angles to the joists
    B. requires approximately the same amount of lumber as subflooring applied at right angles to the joists
    C. requires more lumber than subflooring applied at right angles to the joists
    D. may require more or less lumber than subflooring applied at right angles to the joists, depending on the dimensions of the building

12. A timber laid directly on the ground or on a concrete base to support a floor is called a   12._____

    A. sleeper   B. sizing   C. rail   D. ledger board

13. Diagonal subflooring is preferred to subflooring laid square across the joists because the diagonal subflooring   13.____

    A. stiffens the building
    B. is easier to lay
    C. is more economical to lay
    D. does not require as much nailing

14. A meeting rail is usually found on a   14.____

    A. stair   B. door   C. roof   D. window

15. The size of a sill plate, for a frame building, laid on a continuous concrete wall in the East is USUALLY   15.____

    A. 4" X 6"   B. 4" X 10"   C. 2" X 10"   D. 2" X 8"

16. A valley is made watertight by means of a   16.____

    A. cornice   B. flashing   C. drip sill   D. furring

17. A strip of wood whose purpose is to assist the plasterers to make a straight wall is called a   17.____

    A. casing   B. ground
    C. belt course   D. gauge

18. A hip rafter is framed between   18.____

    A. plate and ridge   B. plate and valley
    C. valley and ridge   D. valley and overhang

19. 2" X 8" rafters are being used on a roof with a pitch of one quarter. The size of ridge board that would MOST PROBABLY be used is   19.____

    A. 2" X 8"   B. 3" X 8"   C. 2" X 10"   D. 2" X 12"

20. When planks intended to be used for roof rafters are not straight, the one of the following statements that is CORRECT is   20.____

    A. all rafters should be erected with the cambers (crown) up
    B. all rafters should be erected with the cambers (crown) down
    C. the rafters should be erected with the cambers (crown) alternately up and down
    D. the plank should not be used for rafters

21.

21.____

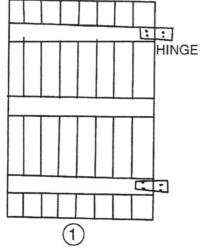

①

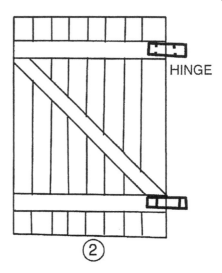

②

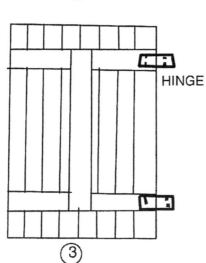

③

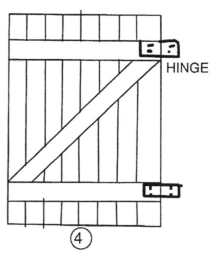

④

The diagram above that shows the BEST method of building a door for a shed is numbered

A. *1* B. *2* C. *3* D. *4*

22. A vertical member separating two windows is called a

22.____

A. muntin B. mullion C. stile D. casing

23. Wood girders framing on a masonry wall in the East should have a MINIMUM bearing of

23.____

A. 2" B. 4" C. 6" D. 8"

24. A collar beam is used to tie

24.____

A. floor joists B. laminated girders
C. roof rafters D. columns

25. Nosing would MOST probably be found in

25.____

A. window frames B. stairs
C. saddles D. scarfs

26. To help prevent plaster cracks when a 2" X 4" stud partition is cut for a doorway, it is USUAL to
      26.____

    A. provide a steel lintel B. use joint   B. hangers
    C. double the header   D. corbel the studs

27. The side support for steps or stairs is called a
      27.____

    A. ledger board   B. pitch board
    C. riser   D. stringer

28. The type of joint MOST FREQUENTLY used where baseboards meet at the corner of a room is a
      28.____

    A. miter   B. mortise and tenon
    C. spline   D. butt

29. The purpose of a water table is to
      29.____

    A. prevent water from entering at the top of a foundation wall
    B. distribute water from a downspout directly on the ground
    C. prevent water from entering a cellar through the cellar floor
    D. prevent water from leaking through a roof at the chimney

30. The one of the following materials that will produce the MOST rigid wall Is _____ sheathing.
      30.____

    A. 1" X 8" horizontal
    B. 1" X 8" diagonal
    C. 29/32" fiberboard
    D. 1/4" plywood

31. Split ring connectors are COMMONLY used to
      31.____

    A. anchor joists to girders
    B. join members of a truss
    C. anchor veneer to framework
    D. connect wood girder to steel column

32. A strike plate would be attached to a
      32.____

    A. sill   B. fascia   C. jamb   D. saddle

33. Blanket insulation is USUALLY placed between
      33.____

    A. siding and sheathing
    B. sheathing and vapor barrier
    C. vapor barrier and rock lath
    D. rock lath and finished plaster

34. A pipe column filled with concrete is called a
      34.____

    A. pintle   B. buttress   C. pilaster   D. lally

35. If you were required to build forms for spandrels, the location of these forms would be at   35.____

    A. footing level between piers
    B. roof level between girders
    C. floor level between columns
    D. footing level over the grillage

36. Where a 2-inch horizontal hole must be made in a 3" X 12" floor joist supporting a uni-   36.____
form live load, the BEST place to make this hole is in the _____ of the joist at the
_____ of the span.

    A. center; end   B. bottom; end
    C. center; center   D. bottom; center

37. To strengthen box corners in new furniture, common practice is to use   37.____

    A. tie rods   B. molly bolts
    C. glue blocks   D. webbing

38. The joint MOST frequently used for attaching the sides of drawers to the fronts is   38.____

    A. mortise and tenon   B. doweled
    C. dovetailed   D. splined

39. The pitch of a roof is one-sixth. If the run is 10 ft., the rise is   39.____

    A. 1'-8"   B. 3'-4"   C. 5'-0"   D. 6'-8"

40. The number of board feet in a 3" X 8", 16 ft. long, is   40.____

    A. 26   B. 28   C. 30   D. 32

41. A right triangle has sides of 5, 12, and 13 inches respectively.   41.____
The area of the triangle, is, in square inches,

    A. 30   B. 32 1/2   C. 60   D. 78

42. The one of the following that would be the dimension used to lay out a right angle is   42.____
_____ feet.

    A. 3, 4, 6   B. 4, 5, 9   C. 6, 8, 10   D. 7, 9, 13

43. A partition wall, with no openings in it, is to be 46 ft. long.   43.____
If studs are spaced 16" o.c. maximum, the number of studs that should be used in this
wall is

    A. 33   B. 34   C. 35   D. 36

44. A flight of stairs has 8 risers. The number of treads it has is   44.____

    A. 7   B. 8   C. 9   D. 10

45. A round post 4 inches in diameter and 4 feet high can carry 12,000 pounds.   45.____
A 6-inch post of the same height, and the same grade and species of wood, can carry
_____ pounds.

    A. 18,000   B. 21,000   C. 24,000   D. 27,000

46. The sum of the following dimensions,
    4'-3 1/4", 3'-2 15/16", 2'-3 1/2", 3'-4 3/4", 4'-7 3/16" is

    A. 17'-9 7/16"   B. 17'-9 1/2"
    C. 17'-9 9/16"   D. 17'-9 5/8"

Questions 47 - 50.

Questions 47 to 50 refer to the sketch below representing the 1st floor plan of a small tool shed.

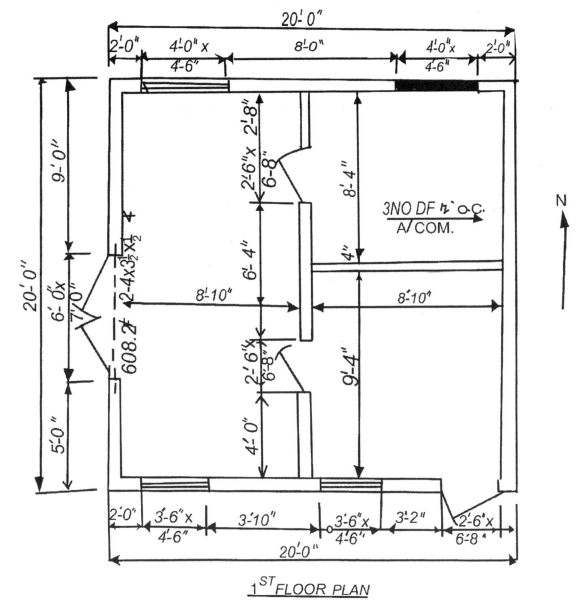

1ST FLOOR PLAN

47. The width* of the windows in the south wall of the building is

    A. 2'-6"   B. 3'-6"   C. 3'-10"   D. 4'-6"

48. The lintel over the large doorway is a   48._____

    A. single wood girder   B. built up wood girder
    C. steel beam and plates   D. steel channel and angles

49. The size of the LARGEST room is   49._____

    A. 8'-10" X 16'-0"   B. 8'-10" X 17'-0"
    C. 8'-10" X 18'-0"   D. 8'-10" X 19'-0"

50. The floor area of the SMALLEST room is, in square feet, MOST NEARLY   50._____

    A. 72   B. 74   C. 76   D. 78

KEY (CORRECT ANSWERS)

1. B	11. C	21. B	31. B	41. A
2. D	12. A	22. B	32. C	42. C
3. D	13. A	23. B	33. B	43. D
4. A	14. D	24. C	34. D	44. A
5. C	15. A	25. B	35. C	45. D
6. A	16. B	26. C	36. C	46. D
7. C	17. B	27. D	37. C	47. B
8. D	18. A	28. D	38. C	48. D
9. D	19. C	29. A	39. B	49. C
10. A	20. A	30. D	40. D	50. B

EXAMINATION SECTION
TEST 1

DIRECTIONS: Each question or incomplete statement is followed by several suggested answers or completions. Select the one that BEST answers the question or completes the statement. *PRINT THE LETTER OF THE CORRECT ANSWER IN THE SPACE AT THE RIGHT.*

1. The specification states: *The value of each change order shall be computed separately by cost of labor and materials, plus equipment allowance, plus overhead and profit.* The MOST probable value of overhead and profit is _____% of the cost of labor and materials plus equipment allowance.

   A. 5   B. 15   C. 34   D. 55

   1.____

2. In the specifications is an item: *Equipment Allowance: Shall include rental of necessary equipment plus 9% of this rental.*
   According to the above specification, if a piece of equipment rents for $35 per day, Equipment Allowance for this equipment rented for 11 days is MOST NEARLY

   A. $484.00   B. $378.42   C. $385.00   D. $419.65

   2.____

3. A supplier quotes a list price of $172.00 less 15 and 10 percent for twelve tools. The ACTUAL cost for these twelve tools is MOST NEARLY

   A. $146   B. $132   C. $129   D. $112

   3.____

4. Which one of the following is the PRIMARY object in drawing up a set of specifications for materials to be purchased?

   A. Control of quality
   B. Outline of intended use
   C. Establishment of standard sizes
   D. Location and method of inspection

   4.____

5. In order to avoid disputes over payments for extra work in a contract for construction, the BEST procedure to follow would be to

   A. have contractor submit work progress reports daily
   B. insert a special clause in the contract specifications
   C. have a representative on the job at all times to verify conditions
   D. allocate a certain percentage of the cost of the job to cover such expenses

   5.____

6. You wish to order sponges in the most economical manner. Keeping in mind that large sponges can be cut up into many smaller sizes, the one of the following that has the LEAST cost per cubic inch of sponge is _____ sponges @ _____.

   A. 2" x 4" x 6"; $.24
   C. 4" x 6" x 36"; $4.80
   B. 4" x 8" x 12"; $1.44
   D. 6" x 8" x 32"; $9.60

   6.____

7. The cost of a certain job is broken down as follows:
   Materials $375
   Rental of equipment   120
   Labor   315
   The percentage of the total cost of the job that can be charged to materials is MOST
   NEARLY _____%.

    A.   40   B.   42   C.   44   D.   46   7._____

8. Partial payments to outside contractors are USUALLY based on the   8._____

    A.   breakdown estimate submitted after the contract was signed
    B.   actual cost of labor and material plus overhead and profit
    C.   estimate of work completed which is generally submitted periodically
    D.   estimate of material delivered to the job

9. Building contracts usually require that estimates for changes made in the field be submit-   9._____
   ted for approval before the work can start.
   The MAIN reason for this requirement is to

    A.   make sure that the contractor understands the change
    B.   discourage such changes
    C.   keep the contractor honest
    D.   enable the department to control its expenses

10. If the cost of a broom went up from $4.00 to $6.00, the percent INCREASE in the original   10._____
    cost is

    A.   20   B.   25   C.   33 1/3   D.   50

11. The AVERAGE of the numbers 3, 5, 7, 8, 12 is   11._____

    A.   5   B.   6   C.   7   D.   8

12. The cost of 100 bags of cotton cleaning cloths, 89 pounds per bag, at 7 cents per pound   12._____
    is

    A. $549.35   B. $623.00   C. $700.00   D. $890.00

13. If 5 1/2 bags of sweeping compound cost $55,00, then 6 1/2 bags would cost   13._____

    A. $60.00   B. $62.50   C. $65.00   D. $67.00

14. The cost of cleaning supplies in a project averaged $330.00 a month during the first 8   14._____
    months of the year.
    How much can be spent each month for the last four months if the total amount that
    can be spent for cleaning supplies for the year is $3,880?

    A. $124   B. $220   C. $310   D. $330

15. The cost of rawl plugs is $2.75 per gross. The cost of 2,448 rawl plugs is   15._____

    A. $46.75   B. $47.25   C. $47.75   D. $48.25

16. A caretaker received $70.00 for having worked from Monday through Friday, 9 A.M. to 5 P.M. with one hour a day for lunch.
The number of hours the caretaker would have to work to earn $12.00 is

    A. 10   B. 6
    C. 70 divided by 12   D. 70 minus 12

16.____

17. Assume that an employee is paid at the rate of $5.43 per hour with time and a half for overtime past 40 hours in a week.
If he works 43 hours in a week, his gross weekly pay is

    A. $217.20   B. $219.20   C. $229.59   D. $241.64

17.____

18. Kerosene costs 36 cents a quart.
At that rate, two gallons would cost

    A. $1.44   B. $2.16   C. $2.88   D. $3.60

18.____

Questions 19-21.

DIRECTIONS: Questions 19 through 21 are to be answered on the basis of the following table.

	Man Days Borough 1		Man Days Borough 2		Man Days Borough 3		Man Days Borough 4	
	Oct.	Nov.	Oct.	Nov.	Oct.	Nov.	Oct.	Nov.
Carpenter	70	100	35	180	145	205	120	85
Plumber	95	135	195	100	70	130	135	80
House Painter	90	90	120	80	85	85	95	195
Electrician	120	110	135	155	120	95	70	205
Blacksmith	125	145	60	180	205	145	80	125

19. In accordance with the above table, if the average daily pay of the five trades listed above is $47.50, the approximate labor cost of work done by the five trades during the month of October for Borough 1 is MOST NEARLY

    A. $22,800   B. $23,450   C. $23,750   D. $26,125

19.____

20. In accordance with the above table, the Borough which MOST NEARLY made up 22.4% of the total plumbing work force for the month of November is Borough

    A. 1   B. 2   C. 3   D. 4

20.____

21. In accordance with the above table, the average man days per month per Borough spent on electrical work for all Boroughs combined is MOST NEARLY

    A. 120   B. 126   C. 130   D. 136

21.____

22. When preparing an estimate for a certain repair job, you determine that $125 worth of materials and 220 man-hours are required to complete the job.
If your man-hour cost is $5.25 per hour, the TOTAL cost of this repair job is

    A. $1,030   B. $1,155   C. $1,280   D. $1,405

22.____

23. Assume that in determining the total cost of a repair job, a 15% shop cost is to be added
to the costs of material and labor.
For a repair job which cost $200 in materials and $600 in labor, the shop cost is

    A. $30   B. $60   C. $90   D. $120

23.____

24. Assume that in quantity purchases, the city receives a discount of 33 1/3%.
If a one gallon can of paint retails at $5.33 per gallon, the cost of 375 gallons of this
paint is MOST NEARLY

    A. $1,332.50   B. $1,332.75   C. $1,333.00   D. $1,333.25

24.____

25. Assume that eight barrels of cement together weigh a total of 3004 lbs. and 12 oz.
If there are four bags of cement per barrel, then the weight of one bag of cement is
HOST NEARLY _____ lbs.

    A. 93.1   B. 93.5   C. 93.9   D. 94.3

25.____

26. Lumber is usually sold by the board foot, and a board foot is defined as a board one foot
square and one inch thick.
If the price of one board foot of lumber is 18 cents and you need 20 feet of lumber 6
inches wide and 1 inch thick, the cost of the 20 feet of lumber is

    A. $1.80   B. $2.40   C. $3.60   D. $4.80

26.____

27. Assume that a trench is 42" wide, 5' deep, and 100' long. If the unit price of excavating
the trench is $35 per cubic yard, the cost of excavating the trench is MOST NEARLY

    A. $2,275   B. $5,110   C. $7,000   D. $21,000

27.____

28. No single activity has a very large effect on the final price of the complete housing structure and, therefore, the total cost is not affected appreciably by the price policy of any
component.
From the above statement, you may conclude that

    A. we cannot hope for substantial reductions in housing costs
    B. the builder must assume responsibility for the high cost of construction
    C. a 10% reduction in the cost of materials would result in much less than a 10%
       reduction in the cost of housing
    D. federal government financing would reduce the city's cost of public housing

28.____

29. Four board feet of lumber, listed at $350 per M, will cost

    A. $3.50   B. $1.40   C. $1.80   D. $4.00

29.____

30. The cost of material is approximately 3/8ths of the total cost of a certain job.
If the total cost of the job is $127.56, then the cost of material is MOST NEARLY

    A. $47.83   B. $48.24   C. $48.65   D. $49.06

30.____

31. It takes four men six days to do a certain job. Working at the same speed, the number of
days it will take three men to do this job is

    A. 7   B. 8   C. 9   D. 10

31.____

32. A contractor on a large construction project USUALLY receives partial payments based on   32.____

    A. estimates of completed work
    B. actual cost of materials delivered and work completed
    C. estimates of material delivered and not paid for by the contractor
    D. the breakdown estimate submitted after the contract was signed and prorated over the estimated duration of the contract

33. In estimating the cost of a reinforced concrete structure, the contractor would be LEAST concerned with   33.____

    A. volume of concrete
    B. surface area of forms
    C. pounds of reinforcing steel
    D. type of coarse aggregate

34. Assume that an employee is paid at the rate of $6.25 per hour with time and a half for overtime past 40 hours in a week.   34.____
If she works 45 hours in a week, her gross weekly pay is

    A. $285.49   B. $296.88   C. $301.44   D. $325.49

35. Cleaning fluid costs $1.19 a quart.   35.____
If there is a 10% discount for purchases over 5 gallons, how much will 8 gallons cost?

    A. $34.28   B. $38.08   C. $42.28   D. $43.43

KEY (CORRECT ANSWERS)

1.	B	11.	C	26.	A
2.	D	12.	B	27.	A
3.	B	13.	C	28.	C
4.	A	14.	C	29.	B
5.	C	15.	A	30.	A
6.	B	16.	B	31.	B
7.	D	17.	D	32.	A
8.	C	18.	C	33.	D
9.	D	19.	C	34.	B
10.	D	20.	B	35.	A
		21.	B		
		22.	C		
		23.	D		
		24.	A		
		25.	C		

TEST 2

DIRECTIONS: Each question or incomplete statement is followed by several suggested answers or completions. Select the one that BEST answers the question or completes the statement. *PRINT THE LETTER OF THE CORRECT ANSWER IN THE SPACE AT THE RIGHT.*

1. When windows are mounted side by side, the vertical piece between them is called the   1.____

   A. muntin   B. casement   C. sash   D. mullion

2. Approximately how many pounds of 16d nails would be required for 1,000 square feet of floor framing area?   2.____

   A. 4-5   B. 7-8   C. 8-10   D. 10-12

3. What is represented by the electrical symbol shown at the right?   3.____

   A. Transformer   B. Buzzer
   C. Telephone   D. Bell

4. Which of the following structures would typically require a relatively higher grade of lumber?   4.____

   A. Vertical stud   B. Joist
   C. Column   D. Mud sill

5. A dump truck with a capacity of 10-12 cubic yards must load, drive, dump, and reposition itself over a 1-mile haul distance.
   What average amount of time should be estimated for this sequence?   5.____

   A. 15 minutes   B. 30 minutes
   C. 1 hour   D. 2 hours

6. The stripping of forms that are to be reused should be charged as   6.____

   A. common labor   B. masonry labor
   C. carpentry labor   D. material credit

7. What type of brick masonry unit is represented by the drawing shown at the right?   7.____
   A. Modular
   B. Norwegian
   C. 3 core
   D. Economy

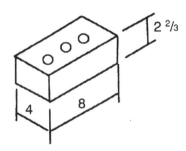

8. Which of the following would be a typical thickness of a crushed-rock base course for an area of asphalt paving?   8.____

   A. 2"   B. 5"   C. 7"   D. 10"

9. Which of the following wood floor materials would be MOST expensive to install? 9.____

   A. Unfinished plank
   B. Walnut parquet
   C. Maple strip
   D. Oak parquet

10. When calculating the air-conditioning needs for a building, a loss factor of _____ should 10.____
    be used for the exposure of walls to common heated surfaces.

    A. 2.0   B. 3.5   C. 6.0   D. 7.5

11. Approximately how many linear feet of moldings, door and window trim, handrails, or 11.____
    similar parts can a carpenter install in a typical work day?

    A. 100   B. 250   C. 400   D. 500

12. Which of the following constructions is NOT typically found in bathroom lavatories? 12.____

    A. Enameled pressed steel
    B. Cast iron
    C. Cast ceramic
    D. Stainless steel

13. What size reinforcing bar is typically used for masonry walls? 13.____

    A. 3   B. 4   C. 7   D. 9

14. Which of the following would NOT be a typical source for a cost-per-square-foot esti- 14.____
    mate?

    A. Architect
    B. Engineer
    C. Appraiser
    D. Building contractor

15. Approximately how many stair treads with risers can a carpenter install in an average 15.____
    work day?

    A. 5-8   B. 10-12   C. 15-18   D. 21-25

16. Each of the following materials is commonly used as sheet metal flashing for roof water- 16.____
    proofing EXCEPT

    A. lead
    B. galvanized steel
    C. copper
    D. zinc

17. The MOST commonly used type of metal lath for wall support is 17.____

    A. self-furring
    B. flat rib
    C. flat diamond mesh
    D. 3/8" rib

18. Approximately how long will it take to install a non-mortised lockset? 18.____

    A. 15 minutes
    B. 30 minutes
    C. 1 hour
    D. 2 hours

19. What is represented by the architectural symbol shown at 19.____
    the right?

    A. Cut stone
    B. Concrete block
    C. Rubble stone
    D. Brick

20. What type of nails are typically used for installing floor sheathing? 20.____

    A. 4d   B. 8d   C. 12d   D. 16d

21. Each of the following is considered *finish* electrical work EXCEPT

    A. outlet boxes
    B. light fixtures
    C. connection of fixtures to wiring
    D. switches

21.____

22. Which component of cost estimating typically presents the GREATEST difficulty?

    A. Materials   B. Overhead
    C. Profit   D. Labor

22.____

23. Approximately how many hours will it take to install and caulk a typical sliding shower door assembly?

    A. 2   B. 4   C. 6   D. 8

23.____

24. What is represented by the electrical symbol shown at the right?

    A. Single pole switch   B. Lock or key switch
    C. Service weather head   D. Main switch

24.____

25. Approximately how many exterior square feet can one painter cover, applying a primer coat and two coats of finish paint, in an average work day?

    A. 100   B. 250   C. 350   D. 500

25.____

KEY (CORRECT ANSWERS)

1.	D		11.	B
2.	B		12.	D
3.	C		13.	B
4.	B		14.	C
5.	B		15.	C
6.	C		16.	A
7.	A		17.	C
8.	B		18.	B
9.	B		19.	A
10.	B		20.	B

21.	A
22.	D
23.	B
24.	A
25.	D

TEST 3

DIRECTIONS: Each question or incomplete statement is followed by several suggested answers or completions. Select the one that BEST answers the question or completes the statement. *PRINT THE LETTER OF THE CORRECT ANSWER IN THE SPACE AT THE RIGHT.*

1. Irregular shapes and narrow lites typically reduce the rate of glass installation by _____%.   1._____

    A. 10-20   B. 25-35   C. 30-50   D. 55-75

2. What is represented by the electrical symbol shown at the right?   —√—   2._____

    A. Exposed wiring   B. Fusible element
    C. Three-way switch   D. Circuit breaker

3. Approximately how many square feet of siding can be installed by a crew in a typical work day?   3._____

    A. 250   B. 500   C. 750   D. 1,000

4. What is the construction term for hinges used on doors?   4._____

    A. Gables   B. Butts   C. Hips   D. Plates

5. Floor joists are typically spaced about _____ apart.   5._____

    A. 16"   B. 2 feet   C. 3 feet   D. 4 feet

6. Which of the following paving materials is generally MOST expensive?   6._____

    A. Brick on sand bed   B. Random flagstone
    C. Asphalt   D. Concrete

7. Approximately how long should it take a 2-person crew to install floor joists for a 100 square-foot area of floor space?   7._____

    A. 30 minutes   B. 1 hour
    C. 3 hours   D. 1 work day

8. A _____ is represented by the mechanical symbol shown at the right.   8._____

    A. pressure-reducing valve   B. motor-operated valve
    C. lock and shield valve   D. globe valve

9. On average, labor costs for a job will be about _____% of the total job cost.   9._____

    A. 15   B. 35   C. 55   D. 85

10. Most exterior paint averages a coverage of about _____ square feet per gallon.   10._____

    A. 100   B. 250   C. 400   D. 550

11. What type of window includes two sashes which slide vertically?   11.____

    A. Double-hung   B. Screen
    C. Casement   D. Sliding

12. Approximately how many linear feet of drywall tape can be applied during an average   12.____
work day?

    A. 250   B. 400   C. 750   D. 1,000

13. What is used to join lengths of copper pipe?   13.____

    A. Molten solder
    B. Threaded ends and sealer
    C. Nipples
    D. Lead-and-oakum seal

14. Typically, one gallon of prepared wallpaper paste will supply adhesive for _____ full rolls   14.____
of wall covering.

    A. 8   B. 12   C. 24   D. 36

15. What is represented by the electrical symbol shown at the right?   15.____

    A. Range outlet
    B. Wall bracket light fixture
    C. Split-wired receptacle
    D. Special purpose outlet

16. What size is MOST wire used in residential work?   16.____

    A. 6   B. 8   C. 12   D. 16

17. Most fire codes require fire-resistant floor underneath fireplace units which extends to at   17.____
least _____ inches beyond the unit.

    A. 6   B. 12   C. 18   D. 24

18. If a building is constructed without a basement, _____ are typically used as footings.   18.____

    A. joists   B. staked caissons
    C. grade beams   D. mud sills

19. What is the MOST commonly used size range for flashing and gutter sheet metal?   19.____

    A. 8-12   B. 14-18   C. 22-26   D. 24-30

20. Approximately how many square feet of interior wall space can one painter, using a   20.____
brush, cover in an hour?

    A. 25-50   B. 100   C. 175-200   D. 250

21. Which of the following downspout materials would be MOST expensive?   21.____

    A. Copper   B. Aluminum
    C. Zinc   D. Stainless steel

22. What is represented by the mechanical symbol shown at the right?   ⊖   22.____

    A. Expansion valve   B. Floor drain
    C. Shower   D. Scale trap

23. Approximately how much lead (pounds) is required per joint in one sewer line lead-and-oakum seal?   23.____

    A. 1/4   B. 1/2   C. 1 1/2   D. 3

24. Which of the following caulking materials is MOST expensive?   24.____

    A. Neoprene   B. Butyl
    C. Polyurethane   D. Latex

25. The assembly inside a tank toilet that controls the water supply is the   25.____

    A. P trap   B. bell-and-spigot
    C. gating   D. ball cock

KEY (CORRECT ANSWERS)

1. C	11. A
2. B	12. A
3. A	13. A
4. B	14. B
5. A	15. C
6. D	16. C
7. C	17. B
8. D	18. C
9. A	19. C
10. C	20. B

21. A
22. A
23. A
24. B
25. C

EXAMINATION SECTION
TEST 1

DIRECTIONS: Each question or incomplete statement is followed by several suggested answers or completions. Select the one that BEST answers the question or completes the statement. *PRINT THE LETTER OF THE CORRECT ANSWER IN THE SPACE AT THE RIGHT.*

1. A maintenance man complains to you that he is getting all the boring jobs to do. You check and find that his complaint has no basis in fact.
   The one of the following which is the MOST likely reason why the maintenance man made such a claim is that he

   A. wants to get even with the supervisor
   B. lives in a world of fantasy
   C. believes the injustice to be real
   D. is jealous of other workers

   1.____

2. When on preliminary review of a mechanic's written grievance you feel the grievance to be unfounded, the FIRST step you should take is to

   A. show the mechanic where he is wrong
   B. check carefully to find out why the mechanic thinks that way
   C. try to humor the mechanic out of it
   D. tell the mechanic to stop complaining

   2.____

3. Assume that you decide to hold a private meeting with one of your mechanics who has a drinking problem that is affecting his work.
   At the meeting, the BEST way for you to handle this situation is to

   A. tell the mechanic off and then listen to what he has to say
   B. criticize the mechanic's behavior to get him to *open up* in order to help him correct his problem quickly
   C. try to get the mechanic to recognize his problem and find ways to solve it
   D. limit the discussion to matters concerning only the problem and look for immediate results

   3.____

4. The one of the following which is a generally accepted guide in criticizing a subordinate EFFECTIVELY is to

   A. criticize the improper act, not the individual
   B. put the listener on the defensive
   C. make the criticism general instead of specific
   D. correct the personality, not the situation

   4.____

5. The one of the following disciplinary methods by which you are MOST likely to be successful in getting a problem employee to improve his behavior is when you

   A. discipline the employee in front of others
   B. consider the matter to be ended after the disciplining
   C. give the exact same discipline no matter how serious the wrongdoing
   D. make an example of the employee

   5.____

6. Of the following statements, the one that is MOST applicable to a disciplinary situation is that discipline should be   6._____

    A. used after a cooling-off period
    B. identical for all employees
    C. consistent with the violation
    D. based on personal feelings

7. The one of the following approaches that is MOST important for you to take in evaluating a mechanic in order to increase his work productivity is to   7._____

    A. first have him evaluate his own performance
    B. meet with him to discuss how he is doing and what is expected on the job
    C. send him a copy of your evaluation of his work performance and give him the opportunity to submit written comments
    D. express in writing your appreciation of his work

8. Assume that you say to one of the mechanics, *Jim, that job you turned out today was top-notch. I didn't think you could do so well with the kind of material you had to work with.*
This statement BEST describes an example of your   8._____

    A. recognition of the man's work
    B. disrespect for the man's feelings
    C. personal favoritism of the man
    D. constructive criticism of the man's work

9. In general, the OUTSTANDING characteristic of employees over 50 years of age is their   9._____

    A. resistance   B. endurance
    C. wisdom   D. job stability

10. You should be interested in the morale of your men because morale is MOST often associated with   10._____

    A. mechanization   B. automation
    C. production   D. seniority regulations

11. Assume that the maintenance work order system is about to be changed. Your workers would MOST likely show the LEAST resistance to this change if you   11._____

    A. downgrade the old maintenance work order system
    B. tell your workers how the change will benefit them
    C. post the notice of the change on the bulletin board
    D. tell the workers how the change will benefit management

12. Of the following, the BEST way to motivate a newly appointed mechanic is to   12._____

    A. explain the meaning of each assignment
    B. make the work more physically demanding
    C. test the mechanic's ability
    D. use as much authority as possible

13. The one of the following which is the LEAST important reason for giving employees information concerning policy changes which will affect them is that employees should know   13.____

    A. why the change is being made
    B. who will be affected by the change
    C. when the change will go into effect
    D. how much savings will be made by the change

14. A foreman who knows how to handle his men will MOST likely get them to produce more by treating them   14.____

    A. alike
    B. as individuals
    C. on a casual basis
    D. as a group

15. Of the following items, the one that a supervisor has the MOST right to expect from his employees is   15.____

    A. liking the job
    B. a fair day's work
    C. equal skill of all mechanics
    D. perfection

16. The one of the following which is the BEST practice for you to follow in handling a dispute between the workers is to   16.____

    A. side with one of the workers so as to end the dispute quickly
    B. pay no attention to the dispute and let the workers settle it themselves
    C. listen to each worker's story of the dispute and then decide how to settle it
    D. discuss the dispute with other workers and then decide how to settle it

17. You are likely to run into an employee morale problem when assigning a dirty job that comes up often.   17.____
Of the following, the BEST method of assigning this work is to

    A. rotate this assignment
    B. assign it to the fastest worker
    C. assign it by seniority
    D. assign it to the least skilled worker

18. Of the following, the one that is generally regarded as the BEST aid to high work productivity of subordinates is a supervisor's skill in   18.____

    A. record keeping
    B. technical work
    C. setting up rules and regulations
    D. human relations

19. The BEST way to help a mechanic who comes to you for advice on a personal problem is to   19.____

    A. listen to the worker's problem without passing judgment
    B. tell the worker to forget about the problem and to stop letting it interfere with his work
    C. talk about your own personal problems to the worker
    D. mind your own business and leave the worker alone

20. You are in charge of the maintenance shop and have learned that within the next two
weeks the maintenance shop will be moved to a new location on the plant grounds, but
you have not learned why this move is taking place. Assume that you have decided not to
keep this information from your mechanics until the reason is known but to inform them
of this matter now.
Of the following, which one is the BEST argument that can be made regarding your
decision?

    A. *Acceptable;* because although the reason is not now known, the mechanics will
eventually find out about the move
    B. *Unacceptable;* because the mechanics do not know at this time the reason for the
move and this will cause anxiety on their part
    C. *Acceptable*; because the mechanics will be affected by the move and they should
be told what is happening
    D. *Unacceptable;* because the mechanics' advance knowledge of the move will tend
to slow down their work output

20._____

21. Of the following, the FIRST action for a foreman to take in making a decision is to

    A. get all the facts
    B. develop alternate solutions
    C. get opinions of others
    D. know the results in advance

21._____

22. Assume that you have just been promoted to foreman.
Of the following, the BEST practice to follow regarding your previous experience at the
mechanic's level is to

    A. continue to fraternize with your old friends
    B. use this experience to better understand those who now work for you
    C. use your old connections to keep top management informed of mechanics' views
    D. forget the mechanics' points of view

22._____

23. You have decided to hold regular group discussions with your subordinates on various
aspects of their duties.
Of the following methods you might use to begin such a program, the one which is
likely to be MOST productive is to

    A. express your own ideas and persuade the group to accept them
    B. save time and cover more ground by asking questions calling for yes or no answers
    C. propose to the group a general plan of action rather than specific ideas carefully
worked out
    D. provide an informal atmosphere for the exchange of ideas

23._____

24. The principle of learning by which a foreman might get the BEST results in training his
subordinates is:

    A. Letting the learner discover and correct his own mistakes
    B. Teaching the most technical part of the work first
    C. Teaching all parts of the work during the first training session
    D. Getting the learner to use as many of his five senses as possible

24._____

25. A new mechanic is to be trained to do an involved operation containing several steps of varying difficulty. This mechanic will MOST likely learn the operation more quickly if he is taught   25.____

    A. each step in its proper order
    B. the hardest steps first
    C. the easiest steps first
    D. first the steps that do not require tools

_____

KEY (CORRECT ANSWERS)

1.	C	11.	B
2.	B	12.	A
3.	C	13.	D
4.	A	14.	B
5.	B	15.	B
6.	C	16.	C
7.	B	17.	A
8.	A	18.	D
9.	D	19.	A
10.	C	20.	C

21.	A
22.	B
23.	D
24.	D
25.	C

_____

TEST 2

DIRECTIONS: Each question or incomplete statement is followed by several suggested answers or completions. Select the one that BEST answers the question or completes the statement. *PRINT THE LETTER OF THE CORRECT ANSWER IN THE SPACE AT THE RIGHT.*

1. The one of the following job situations in which it is better to give a written order than an oral order is when   1._____

    A.   the job involves many details
    B.   you can check the job's progress easily
    C.   the job is repetitive in nature
    D.   there is an emergency

2. Which one of the following serves as the BEST guideline for you to follow for effective written reports?   2._____
Keep sentences

    A.   short and limit sentences to one thought
    B.   short and use as many thoughts as possible
    C.   long and limit sentences to one thought
    D.   long and use as many thoughts as possible

3. Of the following, the BEST reason why a foreman generally should not do the work of an individual mechanic is that   3._____

    A.   the shop's production figures will not be accurate
    B.   a foreman is paid to supervise
    C.   the foreman must maintain his authority
    D.   the employee may become self-conscious

4. One method by which a foreman might prepare written reports to management is to begin with the conclusions, results, or summary and to follow this with the supporting data.   4._____
The BEST reason why management may prefer this form of report is because

    A.   management lacks the specific training to understand the data
    B.   the data completely supports the conclusions
    C.   time is saved by getting to the conclusions of the report first
    D.   the data contains all the information that is required for making the conclusions

5. Forms used for time records and work orders are important to the work of a foreman PRIMARILY because they give him   5._____

    A.   the knowledge of and familiarity with work operations
    B.   the means of control of personnel, material, or job costs
    C.   the means for communicating with other workers
    D.   a useful method for making filing procedures easier

6. The one of the following which is the MOST important factor in determining the number   6._____
   of employees you can effectively supervise is the

   A. type of work to be performed
   B. priority of the work to be performed
   C. salary level of the workers
   D. ratio of permanent employees to temporary employees

7. Of the following, you will be MOST productive in carrying out your supervisory responsi-   7._____
   bilities if you

   A. are capable of doing the same work as your mechanics
   B. meet with your mechanics frequently
   C. are very friendly with your mechanics
   D. get work done through your mechanics

8. You have been asked to prepare the annual budget for your maintenance shop.   8._____
   The one of the following which is the FIRST step you should take in preparing this budget is to determine the

   A. amount of maintenance work which is scheduled for the shop
   B. time it takes for a specific unit of work to be completed
   C. current workload of each employee in the shop
   D. policies and procedures of the shop's operations

9. When determining the amount of work you expect a group of mechanics to perform in a   9._____
   given time, the BEST procedure for you to follow should be to

   A. aim for a higher level of production than that of the most productive worker
   B. stay at the present production level
   C. set general instead of specific goals
   D. let workers participate in the determination whenever possible

10. You have been asked to set next year's performance goals concerning the ratio of jobs   10._____
    completed on schedule to total jobs worked. A review of last year's record shows that the
    workers completed their jobs on schedule 85% of the time, with the best ones showing
    an on-time ratio of 92% and the poorest ones showing an on-time ratio of 65%.
    Using these facts in line with generally accepted goal-setting practices, you should set
    a performance ratio for the next year on the basis of _____ average with a _____
    minimum acceptable for any employee.

    A. 85%; 65%   B. 85%; 70%   C. 90%; 65%   D. 90%; 70%

11. It is important for you to be able to identify the critical parts of a large project such as the   11._____
    remodeling of your maintenance shop.
    The one of the following which is the BEST reason why this is important is that it may

    A. help you to set up good communications between you and your workers
    B. give you a better understanding of the purpose of the project
    C. give you control over the time and cost involved in the project
    D. help you to determine who are your most productive workers

12. When doing work planning for your shop, the factor that you should normally consider LAST among the following is knowing your   12.____

    A. major objectives   B. record keeping system
    C. minor objectives   D. priorities

13. You have the responsibility for ordering all materials for your maintenance shop. A listing   13.____
of materials needed for the operations of your shop is long overdue. You realize that you
are unable to find time to take care of the inventory personally because of a high priority
project you have been working on which has been taking all of your time. You do not
know when you will be finished with the project.
The BEST of the following courses of action to take in handling this inventory matter is
to

    A. request that you be taken off the project immediately so that you may take care of
the inventory
    B. complete your high priority project and then do the inventory yourself
    C. volunteer to work overtime so that you may complete the inventory while continuing
with the project
    D. assign the inventory work to a competent subordinate

14. You have the authority and responsibility for seeing that proper records are kept in your   14.____
shop. Assume that you decide to delegate to a records clerk the responsibility for collect-
ing the time sheets and the authority to make changes on the time sheets to correct the
information when necessary.
Of the following, which one is the BEST argument that can be made regarding your
decision?

    A. *Unacceptable*; because you can delegate only your responsibility but none of your
authority to the records clerk
    B. *Acceptable*; because you can delegate some of your authority and some of your
responsibility to the records clerk
    C. *Unacceptable;* because you can delegate only your authority but none of your
responsibility to the records clerk
    D. *Acceptable;* because you can delegate all your responsibility and all your authority
to the records clerk

15. You will LEAST likely be able to do an effective job of controlling operating costs if you   15.____

    A. eliminate idle time   B. reduce absenteeism
    C. raise your budget   D. combine work operations

16. Of the following actions, the one which is LEAST likely to help in carrying out your   16.____
responsibilities of looking after the interests of your workers is to

    A. crack down on your workers when necessary
    B. let your workers know that you support company policy
    C. prevent the transfers of your workers
    D. back up your workers in a controversy

17. The term *accountability*, as used in management of supervision, means MOST NEARLY   17.____

    A. responsibility for results   B. record keeping
    C. bookkeeping systems   D. inventory control

18. Assume that you have been unable to convince an employee of the seriousness of his poor attendance record by talking to him.
The one of the following which is the BEST course of action for you to take is to

    A. keep talking to the employee
    B. recommend that a written warning be given
    C. consider transferring the employee to another work location
    D. recommend that the employee be fired

18._____

19. When delegating work to a subordinate foreman, you should NOT

    A. delegate the right to make any decisions
    B. be interested in the results of the work, but in the method of doing the work
    C. delegate any work that you can do better than your subordinate
    D. give up your final responsibility for the work

19._____

20. Of the following statements, the BEST reason why proper scheduling of maintenance work is important is that it

    A. eliminates the need for individual job work orders
    B. classifies job skills in accordance with performance
    C. minimizes lost time in performing any maintenance job
    D. determines needed repairs in various locations

20._____

21. Of the following factors, the one which is of LEAST importance in determining the number of subordinates that an individual should be assigned to supervise is the

    A. nature of the work being supervised
    B. qualifications of the individual as a supervisor
    C. capabilities of the subordinates
    D. lines of promotion for the subordinates

21._____

22. Suppose that a large number of semi-literate residents of this city have been requesting the assistance of your department. You are asked to prepare a form which these applicants will be required to fill out before their requests will be considered.
In view of these facts, the one of the following factors to which you should give the GREATEST amount of consideration in preparing this form is the

    A. size of the form
    B. sequence of the information asked for on the form
    C. level of difficulty of the language used in the form
    D. number of times which the form will have to be reviewed

22._____

23. A budget is a plan whereby a goal is set for future operations. It affords a medium for comparing actual expenditures with planned expenditures.
The one of the following which is the MOST accurate statement on the basis of this statement is that

    A. the budget serves as an accurate measure of past as well as future expenditures
    B. the budget presents an estimate of expenditures to be made in the future
    C. budget estimates should be based upon past budget requirements
    D. planned expenditures usually fall short of actual expenditures

23._____

24. A foreman who is familiar with modern management principles should know that the one   24.____
of the following requirements of an administrator which is LEAST important is his ability
to

    A. coordinate work
    B. plan, organize, and direct the work under his control
    C. cooperate with others
    D. perform the duties of the employees under his jurisdiction

25. The one of the following which should be considered the LEAST important objective of   25.____
the service rating system is to

    A. rate the employees on the basis of their potential abilities
    B. establish a basis for assigning employees to special types of work
    C. provide a means of recognizing superior work performance
    D. reveal the need for training as well as the effectiveness of a training program

----

KEY (CORRECT ANSWERS)

1.	A		11.	C
2.	A		12.	B
3.	B		13.	D
4.	C		14.	B
5.	B		15.	C
6.	A		16.	C
7.	D		17.	A
8.	A		18.	B
9.	D		19.	D
10.	D		20.	C

21.	D
22.	C
23.	B
24.	D
25.	A

EXAMINATION SECTION
TEST 1

DIRECTIONS: Each question or incomplete statement is followed by several suggested answers or completions. Select the one that BEST answers the question or completes the statement. *PRINT THE LETTER OF THE CORRECT ANSWER IN THE SPACE AT THE RIGHT.*

1. Assume that a foreman has a new assistant.
   Of the following, the BEST thing for the foreman to do FIRST in order to prepare his assistant to help him with his work and to take over in his absence is to

   A. tell the men that they must give full cooperation to his assistant
   B. assign one of his duties to his assistant and follow-up to see if he does it well
   C. let his assistant know as much as possible about everything he is doing or planning
   D. discuss all matters with his assistant before taking any action

   1._____

2. Of the following, the MOST important reason for the foreman to insist that his workers follow good housekeeping practices is that

   A. a neat and orderly work area will make the foreman look good to his superiors
   B. such tasks represent a good way of keeping the men busy after they have completed their regular assignments
   C. neatness in the working environment will raise the men's morale
   D. good housekeeping is an important element in accident prevention

   2._____

3. Supervising a lazy worker is often very difficult, especially if he is a likeable and capable person.
   Of the following ways a foreman might deal with such a worker, the one which would be LEAST effective in improving his performance would be to

   A. supervise him closely so that the worker will not have the opportunity to neglect his work
   B. give him a job with some responsibility in the hope that this will motivate him to a greater effort
   C. give him unpleasant jobs in order to get him to change his work habits
   D. give him, in a private conference, a firm warning that his laziness cannot be tolerated

   3._____

4. A good foreman supervises his crew completely, even if this means doing some of their work if he can do it better. This statement is GENERALLY

   A. *true*, mainly because a foreman should not make his crew do tasks that he would not do himself
   B. *false*, mainly because the foreman who does this damages his workers' attitude toward the job
   C. *true*, mainly because by watching the foreman the workers can learn how to do a better job
   D. *false*, mainly because the foreman does not have time to do work other than his own

   4._____

5. Assume that you, as foreman, read a new department policy to your employees. Later, you find that they did not understand the policy.
Of the following, the BEST thing for you to do next is to

    A. have the men read the policy and initial it after they read it
    B. write up and distribute an explanation of the policy among the men
    C. arrange a session to explain the policy and allow time for the men to discuss it with you
    D. ask your supervisor to explain the policy to the workers

5.____

6. Assume that, as foreman, you find that one of your men is going about a job in the wrong way.
In criticizing this worker, you should

    A. add some words or phrases to soften the blow while telling him specifically what he is doing wrong
    B. try to be as general as possible so as to spare the feelings of the worker
    C. criticize him strongly and threaten him with disciplinary action so that he won't fall into a habit of making such mistakes
    D. allow him to see the effects of his mistakes so that the criticism will appear justified and well-deserved

6.____

7. For you, as a foreman, to issue written instructions to your men when they have a complicated job to do would be desirable, CHIEFLY because when the men are following written instructions

    A. they can work more quickly
    B. they are less likely to make serious errors in the work
    C. the need for you to inspect the work that they have done would be eliminated
    D. they do not have to make any decisions on their own

7.____

8. The training of new workers is one of the foreman's most important tasks.
In order to introduce a new employee correctly to his job, the one of the following actions a foreman should take FIRST is to

    A. show the new employee the details of his job
    B. explain to the new employee the overall purpose of his job
    C. let the new employee start working on his own, helping him when he asks for it
    D. ask the new employee what type of assignment he would like most

8.____

9. Assume that a foreman has assigned an assistant foreman the responsibility for supervising a job.
Of the following, it is MOST important for him to

    A. give the assistant foreman close supervision to keep him from making obvious mistakes
    B. tell the assistant foreman what jobs to assign to the men who will work with him
    C. give the assistant foreman the authority to make necessary decisions and give orders
    D. require frequent progress reports from the assistant foreman

9.____

10. One of the duties of a foreman is to check the work of his men as it progresses.   10._____
Of the following, the BEST reason for a foreman to inspect work periodically is to

    A.   develop standard work procedures
    B.   check that the work is being done in the most efficient manner
    C.   eliminate the necessity for a final inspection
    D.   watch for slow workers and assign them to other jobs

11. As a foreman, you may find it necessary to obtain the approval of your superior before   11._____
you take action on some matters.
Of the following, the action for which it is MOST important that you obtain such
approval is one that involves

    A.   transferring one of your functions from your unit to another unit
    B.   rotating assignments among your men
    C.   putting one of your men in charge when you expect to be out for a day
    D.   disciplining two men who have had a fight on the job

12. Some foremen issue assignments in the form of requests rather than giving direct orders.   12._____
This practice is GENERALLY

    A.   *poor,* mainly because issuing a request leaves it up to the worker to set the time
        when he will do the task
    B.   *good,* mainly because requesting the worker to do a job permits him to use judg-
        ment in deciding how to do the job
    C.   *poor,* mainly because requests carry less weight than direct orders and imply
        weakness on the part of the foreman
    D.   *good,* mainly because requests carry almost the same weight as a direct order and
        are less likely to offend the worker

13. Assume that, as a newly appointed foreman, you find that the stock distribution system in   13._____
your shop is unsatisfactory and you decide to change it. You then put into effect a new
system which totally changes the old system. This kind of move is USUALLY

    A.   *undesirable,* chiefly because any new system should use the good features of the
        old system as far as possible
    B.   *desirable,* chiefly because attempts to combine features of an old system with
        those of a new system usually do not work out
    C.   *undesirable,* chiefly because you should not throw out the old system until you
        prove that the new one is better
    D.   *desirable,* chiefly because it is always easier to establish a new system than to
        change an old one

14. Assume that you are a foreman and that a new worker in your crew has made an error   14._____
which resulted in injury to another man.
Of the following, the MOST important thing you should do about this incident is to

    A.   have the new worker assigned to different work where accidents are less likely
    B.   study the accident and plan ways of preventing similar accidents
    C.   talk with your entire work crew about the importance of proper safety procedures
    D.   tell the other workers in your crew to be especially careful when working with the
        new man

15. The BEST way for a foreman to keep morale high among his men is to   15._____

    A. give the good workers the best jobs
    B. praise the men when they do a good job
    C. individually assist the men on all their jobs
    D. grant special privileges to those doing good work

16. When a foreman arrives at a job location, he finds that a loud argument is going on between two of his men.
He should FIRST   16._____

    A. send one of the men to another job
    B. find out what caused the argument before deciding what to do
    C. ask one of the other men to tell him the cause of the argument
    D. take the men with him to his boss so that the matter can be settled

17. Assume that you have recently been appointed foreman. Several of the men in your gang, who are good friends of yours, are taking advantage of the situation by slowing down in their work.
As a foreman, you should FIRST   17._____

    A. let it ride since they will probably come around eventually
    B. request that these men be transferred out of your gang
    C. tell them that they must do their work on time
    D. write a note to your boss about what they are doing so that he can take action

18. The BEST action for a foreman to take if one of his men makes a suggestion on how to improve a work procedure is to   18._____

    A. listen to the suggestion and then let the man know as soon as possible if the suggestion can be used
    B. use the suggestion without naming the man who made it since the others in the gang might resent it
    C. tell the man the suggestion is good but say nothing further if you do not think it will work
    D. inform your boss of the suggestion but don't mention the man's name to avoid embarrassing him if the suggestion is turned down

19. The BEST thing for a foreman to do when a new rule comes down from the top which he feels will be unpopular with the men is to   19._____

    A. simply inform the men of the rule without commenting on it
    B. explain the reason for the new rule
    C. announce the rule and tell the men no changes from it will be permitted
    D. explain to the men that he disagrees with the rule, but he can do nothing about it

20. You notice that another foreman is allowing his men to use defective equipment which may eventually result in unnecessary costs and perhaps injury to his men.
The BEST thing for you, as a foreman, to do is to   20._____

    A. discuss the matter with your boss
    B. speak to the other foreman about the matter
    C. speak to the men who are using the unsafe equipment and have them talk to their foreman about the matter
    D. mind your own business and do not interfere with the other foreman

21. Of the following, the one thing that would MOST likely weaken the authority of a foreman   21.____
in the eyes of his men would be

    A. posting a minimum number of rules
    B. periodically reviewing the accepted standards of work and conduct
    C. willingness to listen to suggestions from any of the men
    D. a policy of consulting with his boss on nearly all matters which are of a routine
       nature

22. Assume that you, as a foreman, have told one of your men how to do a certain job. On a   22.____
day when you were absent, your boss comes in to check on the job and gives the man
different orders.
Of the following, it would be BEST for you to

    A. discuss the matter privately with your boss
    B. tell the man that he should have told your boss to see you first
    C. check with your boss before giving orders in the future
    D. tell the men that in the future your orders must be followed without any changes

23. Before a foreman recommends that charges be preferred against one of his men for   23.____
breaking the rules, the foreman should FIRST make absolutely sure that

    A. the charges will be sustained at the hearing
    B. he has all the necessary information on the case
    C. his boss will approve the recommendation
    D. the man's fellow workers will give testimony favorable to the foreman's side of the
       case

24. The BEST way for a foreman to handle a complaint which has little merit is for the fore-   24.____
man to FIRST

    A. start it through the standard grievance procedure
    B. acknowledge the complaint but take no action
    C. warn the man that complaints of this sort make him subject to ridicule
    D. discuss the complaint with the man, pointing out its weakness

25. After having been instructed by your boss how to do a special rush job, you are forced,   25.____
by unforeseen difficulties, to change the method without having time to check with the
boss. When the boss inspects the job, he criticizes you for not doing what he told you.
As a foreman, it would be BEST for you to

    A. complain to the boss's superior
    B. explain the situation to the boss
    C. say nothing but continue to do the job your way after the boss leaves
    D. tell the boss that he is to blame because he was not around when needed

_____

KEY (CORRECT ANSWERS)

1.	C		11.	A
2.	D		12.	D
3.	C		13.	A
4.	B		14.	B
5.	C		15.	B
6.	A		16.	B
7.	B		17.	C
8.	B		18.	A
9.	C		19.	B
10.	B		20.	B

21.	D
22.	A
23.	B
24.	D
25.	B

———

TEST 2

DIRECTIONS: Each question or incomplete statement is followed by several suggested answers or completions. Select the one that BEST answers the question or completes the statement. *PRINT THE LETTER OF THE CORRECT ANSWER IN THE SPACE AT THE RIGHT.*

1. Assume that one of the men asks his foreman to check every step of every job he completes. If the foreman feels that the only reason the man does this is to keep himself *in the clear,* the foreman should

   A. check every job in detail in order to protect himself
   B. refuse to check his work because as a foreman that is his right
   C. avoid the situation by telling the man that he has no time to check the work
   D. tell the man frankly that he is expected to accept some responsibility for what he does.

1.____

2. Assume that one of a foreman's generally reliable men has been doing poor work lately. The BEST thing for the foreman to do FIRST would be to

   A. ask the man whether anything is wrong
   B. tell the man to snap out of it or disciplinary action will be taken
   C. remind the man that he can be brought up on charges
   D. mention that the boss has noticed the man's poor work and doesn't like it

2.____

3. Assume that a new procedure is to be used in carrying out a certain job. The foreman should closely supervise the men using this new procedure in order to

   A. get the work done as quickly as possible
   B. impress his men with the importance of the job
   C. prevent his men from criticizing the new procedure
   D. make certain that his men are familiar with and understand all the details

3.____

4. Good housekeeping in the foreman's work area will CHIEFLY depend upon the

   A. nature of the job
   B. skill of the men assigned
   C. quality of the supervision that the men receive
   D. quality of the material and equipment used

4.____

5. A contractor doing a job for your agency demands to see your boss after accusing you of being prejudiced against him.
   The BEST of the following courses of action for you to follow is to

   A. take him to your boss as he requests
   B. ask him to leave your office if you feel that you are not prejudiced
   C. talk to him until you convince him you are not prejudiced
   D. remind him that you can make trouble for him if he fails to show you proper respect

5.____

6. Of the following courses of action, the BEST one for a foreman to take if one of his men violates a minor safety rule is to

   A. request the rest of the gang to keep an eye on the man
   B. explain to the man how small mistakes can cause serious accidents
   C. point out to the man the only way he will learn is by making mistakes
   D. tell the man that everyone makes small mistakes and not to get upset about it

6.____

7. Employees of an agency should regularly read the bulletin board at their job location MAINLY in order to

    A. learn about any changes in the staff of the agency
    B. learn what previously posted material has been removed
    C. become familiar with new orders and procedures posted on it
    D. show that they have an interest in the business of the agency

7.____

8. Assume that a foreman has just told one of his men how he wants a certain job done. Of the following, the BEST way to make sure that the man knows exactly how the foreman wants the job done is for the foreman to

    A. cross-examine the man
    B. repeat the instructions
    C. reword the instructions
    D. have the man tell him what has to be done and how

8.____

9. Your boss complains to you that he could not find you at your assigned location and that the gang under your supervision was idle while you were away. Of the following, it is MOST important for you to

    A. improve your supervisory practices
    B. explain why you were away
    C. disregard such an unreasonable complaint
    D. make certain you are rarely away from your assigned location

9.____

10. A worker does not fully understand his foreman's instructions and asks for further explanation.
This is

    A. *not desirable;* the foreman's time will be wasted for no reason
    B. *not desirable;* the worker should be able to understand simple instructions
    C. *desirable;* the foreman will be impressed with the worker's interest
    D. *desirable;* proper performance depends on full understanding of the work to be done

10.____

11. Most people like to show what they can do.
Of the following, the job situation where a man would find it MOST difficult to demonstrate his skills and prove his competence is one where

    A. the work is challenging
    B. he is supervised too closely by his foreman
    C. his fellow workers possess the same basic skills as he does
    D. he is called upon frequently to learn new techniques and to operate new equipment

11.____

12. The BEST of the following reasons why a foreman should be familiar with first aid methods is that

    A. someone must be prepared to act quickly in an emergency
    B. the agency may be kept out of a lawsuit if a simple injury is taken care of promptly
    C. money is saved if someone can take care of simple injuries that do not require a doctor
    D. it is sometimes better to do the wrong thing than to do nothing in administering first aid

12.____

13. Assume that a foreman is preparing a report recommending that a standard work proce-   13.____
dure be changed.
Of the following, the MOST important information that he should include in this report
is

    A. a complete description of the present procedure
    B. the details and advantages of the recommended procedure
    C. the type and amount of retraining needed
    D. the percentage of men who favor the change

14. Of the following, the job that is BEST for a foreman to delegate to one of his men is one   14.____
that

    A. is routine
    B. he finds disagreeable
    C. is of a policy-making nature
    D. occupies the greatest percentage of his time

15. Assume that you, the foreman, have been told by your boss that he has discovered a   15.____
serious mistake on one of the jobs that you are in charge of.
The BEST action for you to take is to

    A. tell the boss promptly which one of the men made the mistake
    B. see that the man who made the mistake is not given similar work
    C. accept responsibility for the mistake and correct it
    D. explain that the mistake was made because you have so many new men

16. If a new man frequently reports late for work, his foreman should   16.____

    A. warn him privately that lateness will not be tolerated
    B. have him dropped at the end of his probation period
    C. threaten to transfer him if he continues to come in late
    D. embarrass him in front of the gang so he will break this habit

17. Advance planning of *fill-in* work for his men is helpful to a foreman MAINLY because he   17.____
can use it to

    A. justify a request for more help
    B. show his men the need for speeding up the regular work
    C. prove to his boss that his men do not loaf on the job
    D. keep his men occupied whenever the regular work is delayed

18. The GREATEST advantage of rotating job assignments among the members of a fore-   18.____
man's crew is that rotation

    A. develops workers capable of handling many jobs
    B. insures a full day's work for each man
    C. determines what men are unable to learn new jobs
    D. equalizes the work load

19. A foreman assigning jobs to a group of new workers who have just finished a training course should GENERALLY assign these men to

    A. unimportant jobs since the new workers will probably make mistakes
    B. easy tasks so that the workers will develop a feeling of confidence
    C. jobs normally assigned to more skillful men so that they may learn more quickly
    D. difficult jobs in order to find out how many skills they have learned

19.____

20. Assume that a worker asks his foreman a question about a new maintenance procedure. The foreman is not thoroughly familiar with this procedure.
Of the following, the BEST course of action for the foreman to take is to tell the worker

    A. that he himself must decide which procedure to follow
    B. to ask an experienced mechanic to help him with the job
    C. to go back to the old method
    D. that he does not know the answer but that he will obtain the necessary information

20.____

21. Of the following, the BEST way for a foreman to train one of his new men in a job that the man has not done before is to

    A. show the man a training film about the job
    B. let the man read in the manual about the job
    C. let the man attempt to do the entire job himself under the foreman's personal supervision
    D. assign the man to work with a more experienced man and check his work periodically

21.____

22. In setting up a work schedule for a special job, it is LEAST important for a foreman to know

    A. when the men will be available
    B. the pay rate for the men assigned
    C. the approximate time needed for the job
    D. when the needed material will be available

22.____

23. Assume that you are the foreman and that one of your men has just been injured seriously in an accident.
Your FIRST concern should be

    A. helping the injured man
    B. finding the cause of the accident
    C. reporting the accident to your boss
    D. keeping the rest of your gang working

23.____

24. Of the following jobs, the one which a foreman should generally NOT assign to one of his men to handle is

    A. keeping material and production records
    B. putting the right man on the right job
    C. attending lectures in a safety program
    D. inspecting and maintaining tools and equipment

24.____

25. The LEAST important of the following items to include in an accident report is   25._____

    A. what action you took
    B. why you think the accident took place
    C. the time and place the accident occurred
    D. the equipment or people involved

KEY (CORRECT ANSWERS)

1.	D		11.	B
2.	A		12.	A
3.	D		13.	B
4.	C		14.	A
5.	A		15.	C
6.	B		16.	A
7.	C		17.	D
8.	D		18.	A
9.	A		19.	B
10.	D		20.	D

21.	D
22.	B
23.	A
24.	B
25.	B

TEST 3

DIRECTIONS: Each question or incomplete statement is followed by several suggested answers or completions. Select the one that BEST answers the question or completes the statement. *PRINT THE LETTER OF THE CORRECT ANSWER IN THE SPACE AT THE RIGHT.*

1. Assume that you are told by another foreman that one of your men violated a safety rule. The BEST action for you, as a foreman, to take is to   1._____

   A.   speak to the man about the incident
   B.   tell the other foreman to leave your men alone
   C.   watch this man closely in order to catch him next time
   D.   give your entire gang a strong talk on safety procedures

2. Of the following, the MAIN purpose of a safety training program is to   2._____

   A.   fix the blame for accidents
   B.   describe accidents which have occurred
   C.   maintain job progress under unsafe working conditions
   D.   make the men aware of the basic causes of accidents

3. The MAIN reason for overhauling machines on a regular basis is to   3._____

   A.   provide good training for the men
   B.   make work for slack times
   C.   minimize costly breakdowns
   D.   use spare parts before they deteriorate

4. The MOST important reason for the requirement that every department operate within a budget is that a budget will   4._____

   A.   enable spending to be controlled in advance
   B.   clearly define the area of responsibility of a department
   C.   enable a department to cut down on provisional appointments
   D.   establish a good base for comparing this year's activities with last year's

5. The rules and regulations of an agency are usually LEAST useful in   5._____

   A.   encouraging safe practices
   B.   relieving the foremen of their supervisory responsibilities
   C.   providing a fair basis for any necessary disciplinary action
   D.   helping the men in the proper performance of their duties

6. The morale of employees depends to a great extent on whether they are able to influence decisions made by management on matters that directly affect the employees. On the basis of this statement, the one of the following situations which will do the MOST to raise morale is when   6._____

   A.   the workers have recently received a scheduled pay raise
   B.   a suggestion made by a group of workers has resulted in a change in an established procedure
   C.   the supervisory staff decides to hold periodic conferences with individual workers to discuss their performance
   D.   a department head makes regular visits to job sites to show his interest in each phase of the department 's operations

7. Proper training encourages employees to cooperate and lowers operating costs.   7._____
The statement MOST consistent with this statement is that

    A. training is only useful if costs can be lowered
    B. new workers get more benefit out of training than old employees
    C. training is a factor in improving morale and efficiency
    D. employees will refuse to cooperate if they do not receive proper training

8. The BEST of the following reasons for submitting written accident reports as soon as   8._____
possible after the occurrence of an accident is that

    A. a person would tend to include too much detail after a long delay
    B. a person can more accurately recall an event which is fresh in his mind
    C. it is easier to recall events in their proper relationship after a lapse of time
    D. an experienced person can easily recall all essential detail after a long delay

9. In order for a foreman to get the work done, his orders to his men must be effective.   9._____
To make sure that the orders to his men will be most effective, a foreman should

    A. tell his men the reasons why every order must be given
    B. include a great amount of detail in most orders
    C. make the orders very brief in order to keep the attention of the men
    D. give the orders and then make some checks to see if the men understand them

10. The MOST valid reason why a particular job might have a time limit set on it is that   10._____

    A. the men will be kept continuously busy
    B. this particular job is urgent
    C. maximum output can be achieved only in this way
    D. the best quality of work is thus obtained

11. If a foreman assigns an assistant foreman to supervise a group of substitute laborers   11._____
temporarily, it would be MOST important for him to describe carefully to the assistant
foreman the

    A. previous work experience of each substitute laborer
    B. length of time the assignment is likely to last
    C. nature and extent of the supervisory duties to be assumed
    D. reasons why substitute employees are not so dependable as regular employees

12. Suppose that your superior informs you that several of your men have complained to him   12._____
about your *unusually strict supervisory methods.*
In this situation, it would be BEST for you to

    A. ask your superior whether it is fair for him to let the men go over your head with
       complaints
    B. ask your superior if the men have given him any specific examples of your *strict
       supervisory methods*
    C. tell your superior that you are just doing your job
    D. tell your superior that you will try to ease up

13. If an experienced subordinate comes to you for a decision about a problem that he has full authority and the necessary knowledge to solve himself, it would generally be BEST for you to

    A. discuss with him the several alternative solutions to the problem and instruct him to make the decision himself
    B. make the decision but advise him that if this comes up again in the future he must make the decision himself
    C. make the decision without further comment
    D. refuse to discuss the matter and advise him that it is his responsibility to handle this himself

13.____

14. At a private conference, your superior discusses with you the failure of your section to keep up with schedules.
He remarks that he believes you are saddled with a poor group of men and he suggests you *push them harder* to get the work done. You sincerely believe that you and your force have done the best possible job with the men and equipment available.
In this situation, you should

    A. assume full responsibility and blame since you are the boss of the section
    B. explain the circumstances and point out why you feel that you and the men are doing a good job
    C. suggest to your superior that he himself speak to the men about the problem
    D. tactfully remind your superior that you are closer to the problem than he is

14.____

15. The number of subordinates directly reporting to a superior should not be greater than he can supervise competently.
This is an acceptable definition of

    A. chain of command   B. span of control
    C. specialized functions   D. unity of command

15.____

16. Assume that your superior has issued orders for a change in work procedures that your men disagree with.
As a foreman, it would be BEST for you to tell your men that

    A. nothing can be done about it at this time, even if their complaints are justified
    B. they should complain to your superior, not to you
    C. you didn't like the changes yourself and tried to talk your superior out of them
    D. you will take up their complaints with your superior

16.____

17. Suppose you are going to train your men on a new piece of equipment.
In planning your course of instruction, to which one of the following questions should you give FIRST consideration?

    A. Exactly what do I want the men to learn in this course?
    B. How much time should I devote to this instruction?
    C. What assistance can I get in running this training program?
    D. What is the background of the men whom I will instruct?

17.____

18. You can pass the buck up but you can't pass it down. This statement implies MOST   18._____
directly that a foreman

    A. is not responsible for the acts of his subordinates
    B. is responsible for the acts of his subordinates
    C. is responsible for the acts of his superiors
    D. must take the blame for anything he does wrong

19. A good foreman should know when to refer a matter to his superior and when to handle it   19._____
himself.
Of the following, the situation which a foreman would MOST appropriately refer to his
superior is

    A. poor cooperation by a storekeeper in his section
    B. a complaint about poor collection service in the section
    C. a disagreement between two of his men
    D. a breakdown of recently purchased department equipment

20. If, after you have been a foreman for several years, you find that your men never com-   20._____
plain to you about working conditions or assignments, this is MOST probably a sign that

    A. there is poor communication between you and your men
    B. the men are interested mainly in their rate of pay
    C. the men have nothing to complain about
    D. you are a very good officer

21. In hearings involving employees charged with violations, one of the main breaches of   21._____
discipline is failing to obey orders.
The CHIEF implication this should have for the foreman is that he should

    A. issue orders in writing whenever this is practicable
    B. make assignments to *teams* of men as often as possible so that the men in a team
       can check each other
    C. make sure his orders are understood and check on their implementation as soon
       as possible
    D. take disciplinary action promptly for failure to obey orders

22. Suppose that work by your men in the field is sometimes delayed because they wait for   22._____
you to arrive to make certain decisions before continuing with their work.
As a foreman, this should indicate to you the need for

    A. breaking up job assignments into smaller units
    B. developing more initiative in your men
    C. having the men select someone to be in charge if you are not there
    D. issuing complete instructions if you know you are going to be away

23. Before you turn in a report you have written of an investigation that you have made, you   23._____
discover some additional information you didn't know about before.
Whether or not you rewrite your report to include this additional information should
depend MAINLY on the

    A. amount of time remaining before the report is due
    B. established policy of the department covering the subject matter of the report
    C. bearing this information will have on the conclusions of the report
    D. number of people who will eventually review the report

24. When a foreman submits a periodic report to the district office, he should realize that the   24._____
CHIEF importance of such a report is that it

    A. is the principal method of checking on the efficiency of the officer and his subordi-
nates
    B. is something to which frequent reference will be made
    C. eliminates the need for any personal follow-up or inspection by higher echelons
    D. permits the agency head to exercise his functions of direction, supervision, and
control better

25. Conclusions and recommendations are usually better placed at the end rather than at   25._____
the beginning of a report because

    A. the person preparing the report may decide to change some of the conclusions
and recommendations before he reaches the end of the report
    B. they are the most important part of the report
    C. they can be judged better by the person to whom the report is sent after he reads
the facts and investigations which come earlier in the report
    D. they can be referred to quickly when needed without reading the rest of the report

———————

KEY (CORRECT ANSWERS)

1.	A	11.	C
2.	D	12.	B
3.	C	13.	A
4.	A	14.	B
5.	B	15.	B
6.	B	16.	D
7.	C	17.	A
8.	B	18.	B
9.	D	19.	D
10.	B	20.	A

21.	C
22.	B
23.	C
24.	D
25.	C

EXAMINATION SECTION
TEST 1

DIRECTIONS: Each question or incomplete statement is followed by several suggested answers or completions. Select the one that BEST answers the question or completes the statement. *PRINT THE LETTER OF THE CORRECT ANSWER IN THE SPACE AT THE RIGHT.*

1. One of your subordinates, whom you consider to be a troublemaker because of his poor attitude toward his work, has been complaining to other employees about his work and stirring them up to make similar complaints. For you to respond to his actions discreetly and impersonally without any show of emotion or upset is considered to be   1.____

   A. *good* practice; you may change his attitudes for the better
   B. *good* practice; he may be so frustrated by your reaction that he will request a transfer
   C. *poor* practice; other employees may follow his example and choose him as their spokesman
   D. *poor* practice; he may not know how to respond to your lack of emotion

2. The practice of a foreman's requesting his subordinates to submit suggestions regarding ways of reducing costs is   2.____

   A. *inadvisable;* reducing costs is the foreman's responsibility, not that of his subordinates
   B. *inadvisable* he may waste a great deal of time by having to review worthless suggestions
   C. *advisable;* it will give subordinates something to do when they have no work to occupy them
   D. *advisable;* asking subordinates for ideas on cost reduction will make them feel more involved in the work process

3. Of the following, which is the BEST way to store steel pipe and other similarly shaped metal pieces?   3.____

   A. Stack in layers, with alternating rows of materials placed lengthwise and widthwise
   B. Stack in a pyramid shape, with sheets of wood placed between the layers
   C. Stack in layers, with strips of iron, the ends of which are turned up, placed between the layers
   D. In vertical rows, upright against a wall

4. Which one of the following is NOT a usual hazard of handling and servicing storage batteries?   4.____

   A. Acid burns   B. Bruised knuckles
   C. Lead poisoning   D. Electric shock

5. As a foreman, at which point should you report an employee to your superior for working in an unsafe manner?   5.____

   A. The first time he does something that endangers himself or another employee
   B. Usually not at all; this is a matter that should be handled by the foreman
   C. When you become aware of a pattern of unsafe operations in his work
   D. When an accident occurs

6. In order to prevent a fire, oily work rags should be   6._____

    A. kept in covered metal containers
    B. kept in neat piles in a well-ventilated area
    C. kept in open storage boxes, at least ten feet away from any flammable material
    D. wrapped in newspaper and stacked neatly against a fireproof wall

7. For which one of the following uses would it be UNSAFE to use a carpenter's hammer?   7._____
Striking a

    A. casing nail   B. hand punch
    C. hardened steel surface   D. plastic surface

8. When a certain gasoline tank is filled to capacity, it holds 420 gallons.   8._____
If it is 3/4 full, the number of gallons of gasoline it is holding is

    A. 280   B. 315   C. 360   D. 375

9. Eight men working full time take 16 days to do a job. How long should it take if four men   9._____
do this job? _____ days.

    A. 26   B. 28   C. 32   D. 38

10. If 20 feet of lumber costs $62.00, the cost of 45 feet would be   10._____

    A. $136.25   B. $139.50   C. $144.25   D. $149.50

11.   11._____

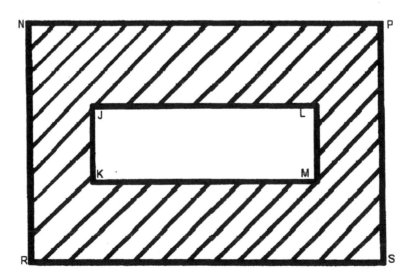

Shown above is a rectangle (JKLM) inside another rectangle (NPSR). What is the area
of the shaded portion if LM measures 20 feet, JL measures 30 feet, NR measures 45
feet, and RS measures 55 feet?
_____ square feet.

    A. 600   B. 975   C. 1,875   D. 2,475

12. To produce a certain cleaning compound, four materials, W, X, Y, and Z, are combined by mixing 6 pounds of W, 5 pounds of X, 3 pounds of Y, and 1 pound of Z.
In order to make up 270 pounds of this cleaning compound, the number of pounds of W required is _____ pounds.

    A. 100   B. 108   C. 112   D. 120

12.____

13. The normal work week for a laborer is 35 hours.
If a laborer spends 27 hours at Job Location A and the rest of his work week at Job Location B, the percentage of time spent at Job Location B is MOST NEARLY _____ percent.

    A. 19   B. 21   C. 23   D. 25

13.____

14. Which one of the following is the GENERALLY recommended method of assigning work to your subordinates?

    A. Jobs are given to each man according to his ability to perform the job.
    B. Jobs that take the shortest time are given to the workers with the greatest seniority.
    C. The same amount of work is distributed to each man all of the time.
    D. Least important jobs are given to the less experienced workers.

14.____

15. Which one of the following tasks USUALLY requires two men to work together until the task is completed?

    A. Removing glass partitions from one location and reinstalling them in another
    B. Repairing a leaking faucet
    C. Filling requisitions from stock bins
    D. Clearing walkways of ice and snow

15.____

Questions 16–17.

DIRECTIONS: Questions 16 and 17 are to be answered on the basis of the following report.

To: Al Forbes   Date: March 30
     Director, Building Maintenance

                                   Subject:

From: Jim Harris
     Foreman

On March 30, at 10:30 A.M., while working on a piece of sheet metal in the machine shop, Steve Farrell cut his hand so badly that he was rushed to the hospital and required 10 stitches. After the accident, it was determined that Steve had not been wearing gloves when the accident occurred. It is, therefore, suggested that safety procedures for materials handling be reviewed so that an accident such as this may be prevented in the future.

16. The subject of the report has been left out.
Which of the following would be BEST as the subject of this report?

    A. Dangerous Conditions in the Machine Shop
    B. Carelessness of Employees Working in the Machine Shop
    C. Procedures for Handling Accidents
    D. Report of Accident Due to Unsafe Materials Handling

16.____

17. Of the following, this report is unsatisfactory because it omits   17.____

    A.   a recommendation for disciplinary action against Steve Farrell
    B.   details regarding how the accident occurred
    C.   Steve Farrell's prior accident record
    D.   the number of sick days that Steve Farrell has available

18. Suppose an employee under your supervision appears to be developing the habit of   18.____
wandering off for a half-hour or more almost every afternoon without offering any
explanation.
The FIRST thing you should do in this situation is to

    A.   assign extra work to the employee so that he will have no time to wander off
    B.   reprimand the employee officially and give him a copy of the reprimand
    C.   transfer the employee to another type of work and observe if his behavior remains
        the same
    D.   talk to the employee about the reasons why he is leaving the job site

19. Of the following, the MAIN advantage of having one employee responsible for the issu-   19.____
ance of tools is

    A.   it assures that the right tool will be used for a particular job
    B.   tools will be less likely to be damaged
    C.   it insures accountability for the tools
    D.   it discourages the use of an employee's personal tools

20. After being inspected, a new ladder is usually coated with a preservative such as clear   20.____
varnish.
Of the following, the MAIN reason for using a clear preservative is that

    A.   the name of the department imprinted on the ladder can be easily identified
    B.   defects occurring after the inspection can be easily noticed
    C.   workers using the ladder are likely to maintain a new ladder in good condition
    D.   cracks in the ladder are less likely to occur than if the ladder were painted

KEY (CORRECT ANSWERS)

1.	A	11.	C
2.	D	12.	B
3.	C	13.	C
4.	C	14.	A
5.	C	15.	A
6.	A	16.	D
7.	C	17.	B
8.	B	18.	D
9.	C	19.	C
10.	B	20.	B

TEST 2

DIRECTIONS: Each question or incomplete statement is followed by several suggested answers or completions. Select the one that BEST answers the question or completes the statement. *PRINT THE LETTER OF THE CORRECT ANSWER IN THE SPACE AT THE RIGHT.*

1. Assume that you, a foreman, expect that some of your workers will have an objection to an order that you must issue.
   If it is not an emergency order, it is MOST advisable for you to

   A. explain to your workers that you do not agree with the order, but that you have no power to do anything but follow it
   B. issue the order without comment and discourage discussion or objections by your workers
   C. state and explain the order carefully to your workers and allow them time to ask questions and to discuss with you their objections
   D. warn your workers before issuing the order that you will take disciplinary action against anyone who resists carrying out the order

   1._____

2. On the job, practical jokes have been played frequently upon one particular man under your supervision. When you, as a foreman, ask the reason for such behavior by the men who play these tricks, they say they do this because the victim invites these tricks upon himself.
   Of the following, it is MOST appropriate for you, the foreman, to FIRST

   A. warn each man involved in such acts that these practical jokes must be discontinued immediately
   B. post a written notice addressed to all the men under your supervision warning them of the dangers involved in playing practical jokes
   C. review the work schedule of your subordinates to see that they have enough work to occupy them for a full day
   D. ask the man on whom the tricks were played if he resents being the victim of such tricks

   2._____

3. Under which one of the following circumstances would it be BEST for a foreman to give orders in the form of commands rather than requests?
   When a foreman

   A. is giving orders to one employee directly rather than to the entire crew
   B. is giving orders that require additional instructions as the work progresses
   C. is giving orders to his entire crew to cope with a critical situation
   D. has been ordered by his supervisor to furnish a skeleton crew for holiday work

   3._____

4. When carrying objects on a two–wheeled handtruck, placing the heavier objects on the bottom of the load is a

   A. *good* practice, because the lighter objects are less likely to be damaged
   B. *poor* practice, because the lighter objects are more likely to fall off
   C. *good* practice, because more weight can be loaded on the truck
   D. *poor* practice, because it will be harder to start the truck in motion

   4._____

5. Of the following, the MAIN advantage in using a Phillips head screw is that

    A. the threads of the Phillips head screw have a deeper bite than standard screw threads

    B. the screwdriver used on this type of screw is more likely to keep its edge than a standard screwdriver

    C. a single screwdriver fits all size screws of this type

    D. the screwdriver used on this type of screw is less likely to slip than a standard screwdriver

5._____

6. One of the reasons why a polyester rope is considered to be the BEST general-purpose rope is that it _____ ropes made of other materials.

    A. does not stretch as much as

    B. is available in longer lengths than

    C. does not fray as much as

    D. contains more strands than

6._____

7. A daily inspection tour by the foreman would be of GREATEST benefit to him and his subordinates when the subordinates realize that the foreman

    A. is available to answer any questions they might have about the work

    B. is checking up on them to make certain they are not wasting time

    C. is looking for the type of work that will bring his name to the attention of his superiors

    D. will lend a hand to get the daily work accomplished

7._____

8. For you to use different methods of discipline for each employee is considered to be

    A. *good* practice; each employee should be disciplined in a manner that is most effective for him

    B. *good* practice; your employees will be afraid to misbehave because they can no longer predict your behavior

    C. *poor* practice, employees may consider these different methods a sign of indecisiveness and lose respect for you

    D. *poor* practice; an employee who believes he is getting the harshest discipline may become hostile and antagonistic

8._____

9. As a foreman, you have just informed your crew that you want them to follow a new procedure when signing out for tools from the tool cabinet.
Of the following, the MOST efficient method for you to adopt to make certain that your crew is reminded of this new procedure is to

    A. take each man aside and tell him you are counting on him to follow the correct procedure

    B. announce to the men that all tools in the cabinet are stamped with a serial number and the agency name

    C. post instructions for the new procedure at the tool cabinet so the men will be sure to see then when requisitioning tools

    D. question the men at their work sites to learn whether they obtained the tools by following the new procedure

9._____

10. For you as a foreman to tell an individual employee how much he is expected to do on a job assignment is a   10.____

    A. *good* practice, because he will have a goal to try to reach
    B. *bad* practice, because he will be able to determine if you are giving others the same amount of work
    C. *good* practice, because you will be able to give the individual more detailed instructions on how to do the job
    D. *bad* practice, because he will do the minimum amount of work and not be motivated to continue further

11. A laborer who has worked in your agency for five years has just been transferred into your unit.   11.____
In order for you to be able to plan his assignments properly, the FIRST thing you should do is to

    A. ask him what he already knows about the work handled in your unit
    B. plan a training program for him in which all phases of your unit's operations are covered
    C. assign one of your more experienced laborers to train him in the work of your unit
    D. tell him what you want him to do and then interview him

12. After you have assigned a job to one of your workers, he complains to your superior about the job instead of coming to you with his complaint. He recognizes that it is proper to discuss the complaint with you first. However, he points out that in the past other employees under your supervision have successfully bypassed you with their complaints. Which of the following approaches generally would be MOST productive in getting your subordinates to turn to you first with their complaints?   12.____

    A. Ask your superior how he handled this complaint, so that you can handle it in the same way when the complaint arises again.
    B. Clarify the steps of the complaint procedure with your employees.
    C. Ask your superior to take no action on the employee complaints, but to refer the employee to you, their supervisor.
    D. Tell your employees that if they do not bring the complaints to you first, they cannot take them to your superior.

13. Of the following, the MAIN reason that on-the-job training is widely used is that   13.____

    A. the trainee can be producing while he is being trained
    B. the supervisor can assign several trainees to the training at one time
    C. the trainee can progress at his own speed
    D. most supervisors are well-qualified to conduct on-the-job training

14. Of the following, it is BEST for a foreman to begin a new employee's training right after the new employee has

    A. made several errors in performing the first task he has been given to do
    B. had an opportunity to meet all the other employees having his title
    C. reported for work in the unit
    D. shown an interest in learning more about the job he has been doing

14.____

15. As a foreman, you have always handwritten accident reports. However, a new accident reporting procedure requests that you use a printed form which asks specific questions and provides blank spaces where the information about the accident can be filled in.
Of the following, the MOST important advantage of using this printed form is that

    A. the information can be completed by any one of your workers if you are not available
    B. your supervisor can rely on information in a printed form to be more reliable than a completely handwritten report
    C. you can enter as much or as little information on the form as you think necessary
    D. you will be less likely to omit needed information

15.____

16. If you replace a blown fuse, and the replaced fuse has burned out shortly thereafter, the FIRST step that should be taken when the replaced fuse has been damaged is that

    A. this second fuse should be replaced by a new fuse of the same type and amperage
    B. this second fuse should be replaced by a new fuse of slightly greater amperage
    C. the circuit should be disconnected while the cause of the burn–out is determined
    D. a check of all other fuses at the electrical connection should be made to determine if they were in working order

16.____

17. When you are placing a 12-foot portable ladder with a non-slip base against the side of a building, the distance from the base of the ladder to the base of the side of the building should be MOST NEARLY, according to general safety rules, _____ feet.

    A. 2   B. 3   C. 4   D. 6

17.____

18. A foreman must supply sufficient plywood paneling, each panel measuring 4 feet by 8 feet, to erect a three–sided barrier fence 8 feet high in front of a building entrance. This rectangular area will be closed to the public while the building alterations are made. The longer side of the area measures 24 feet, and each of the shorter sides measures 12 feet.
The MINIMUM number of plywood panels necessary to erect this fence is

    A. 9   B. 12   C. 18   D. 24

18.____

19. The proper saw to use to cut wood with the grain is a _____ saw.

    A. hack   B. crosscut   C. back   D. rip

19.____

20. One of your men, Tom Jones, has shown up late for work several times in the past two   20.____
weeks. The quality of his work, however, is good. This morning, Jones comes in late
again.
Of the following, the FIRST action you should take is to

    A. warn Jones that if his lateness continues he will be disciplined
    B. send Jones to the Personnel Officer for disciplinary action
    C. speak to your own supervisor and ask him what to do in this case
    D. ask Jones why he has been arriving late for work so often lately

———

KEY (CORRECT ANSWERS)

1.	C		11.	A
2.	A		12.	C
3.	C		13.	A
4.	A		14.	C
5.	D		15.	D
6.	A		16.	C
7.	A		17.	B
8.	A		18.	B
9.	C		19.	D
10.	A		20.	D

———

READING COMPREHENSION
UNDERSTANDING AND INTERPRETING WRITTEN MATERIAL

EXAMINATION SECTION
TEST 1

DIRECTIONS: Each question or incomplete statement is followed by several suggested answers or completions. Select the one that BEST answers the question or completes the statement. *PRINT THE LETTER OF THE CORRECT ANSWER IN THE SPACE AT THE RIGHT.*

Questions 1-4.

DIRECTIONS: Questions 1 through 4 refer to the following paragraph.

Hot hide glue is an excellent adhesive, but it is generally not used by the home handy-man. You can buy hide glue in cake, flake, or ground forms. Soak the glue in lukewarm water overnight, following the manufacturer's instructions. Use glass ovenware or metal containers, double-boiler fashion, to keep it below 150° F. and apply hot. Heat only the quantity needed; frequent reheating weakens the glue. It sets fast, but requires tight clamping and matched joints for proper bonding.

1. According to the paragraph, the number of forms in which hide glue can be bought is   1.____

   A. 2   B. 3   C. 4   D. 5

2. According to the above paragraph, hide glue should   2.____

   A. be used only by the home handyman
   B. be boiled twice
   C. never be used by the home handyman
   D. be prepared according to manufacturer's instructions

3. According to the above paragraph, frequent reheating of hide glue   3.____

   A. makes it set fast   B. weakens it
   C. keeps it below 150° F   D. is desirable

4. The one of the following which is the MOST appropriate title for the above paragraph is   4.____

   A. TIPS FOR THE HOME HANDYMAN
   B. PREPARATION AND USE OF HIDE GLUE
   C. WHAT IS HIDE GLUE?
   D. REPAIR OF GLASS OVENWARE AND METAL CONTAINERS

Questions 5-9.

DIRECTIONS: Questions 5 through 9 are based on the paragraph below. Use only the information contained in this paragraph in answering these questions.

Common nails and brads are designated by the letter *d,* indicating *penny;* thus 8d = 8 penny. In order to determine the length required of a nail in pennies, the thickness of the board to be penetrated, for example, 25/32 of an inch, is multiplied by 8. Then, 11/2 is added to the result, which in this instance indicates an 8d nail: (25/32 x 8 = 61/4 + 11/2=73/4= 8).

To reverse the computation, when only the penny size is known, to determine the length in inches (up to 10d), the penny size is divided by 4 then 1/2 is added. For example, an 8d nail measures 2 1/2 inches because 8 ÷ 4 = 2 + 1/2=2 1/2.

5.   The letter used to designate common nails and brads is   5._____

    A. a   B. b   C. c   D. d

6.   To penetrate a board 15/16" thick, the length of nail required, in pennies, is   6._____

    A. 8   B. 9   C. 10   D. 11

7.   The length of a 6 penny nail, in inches, is   7._____

    A. 2   B. 3   C. 4   D. 5

8.   The word *penetrated,* as used in the above paragraph, means MOST NEARLY   8._____

    A. congealed   B. dulled
    C. hanged   D. pierced

9.   The word *designated,* as used in the above paragraph, means MOST NEARLY   9._____

    A. considered   B. driven
    C. named   D. probed

Questions 10-17.

DIRECTIONS: Questions 10 through 17 are based on the paragraph below. Use only the information contained in this paragraph in answering these questions.

Lumber is measured according to a system known as board measure (bm). The unit is a board foot, which is equal in volume to a board 1 foot wide, 1 foot long, and 1 inch thick, or 144 cubic inches. To compute board measure, if the board is less than 1 inch thick, consider the fraction as a full inch. If it is thicker than 1 inch, however, figure the inches and fractions of an inch exactly. Thus, a 1/2 inch board is considered as 1 inch thick bm, but a 1 1/2 inch board as 1 1/2 inches. To compute board feet, multiply the length of the board, in feet, by the width, in feet, and multiply this product by the thickness in inches.

10.   The unit of measuring lumber is a   10._____

    A. ampere   B. board foot
    C. milligram   D. pound per square inch

11.   Lumber is measured according to a system known as   11._____

    A. board measure   B. cubic capacity
    C. linear feet   D. logarithms

12. A board foot is equal to   12.____

    A. 144 cubic inches   B. 3 linear feet
    C. 4 by 8 feet   D. 72 cubic inches

13. If a piece of lumber is 3/4" thick, in computing board measure, its thickness will be considered as   13.____

    A. 4"   B. 3/4"   C. 1"   D. 1 1/2"

14. If a piece of lumber is 1 3/4" thick, in computing board measure, its thickness will be considered as   14.____

    A. 1/2"   B. 1"   C. 1 1/2"   D. 1 3/4"

15. The number of board feet in a board 12 feet long by 18 inches wide by 1/2 inch thick is   15.____

    A. 9   B. 18   C. 108   D. 216

16. The number of board feet in a board 12 feet long by 18 inches wide by 1 3/4 inches thick is   16.____

    A. 18   B. 31.5   C. 216   D. 270

17. The word *compute,* as used in the above paragraph, means MOST NEARLY   17.____

    A. add   B. calculate   C. divide   D. subtract

Questions 18-24.

DIRECTIONS: Questions 18 through 24 are based on the paragraph below. Use only the information contained in this paragraph in answering these questions.

    Screws can be purchased in lengths varying fro1/4" to 6". Lengths from 1/4" to 1" increase by 1/8" units; those from 1" to 3" by 1/4" units; and from 3" to 5" by 1/2" units. They come with flat, round, or oval heads, the flat head type being used for countersinking. Soaping the screw first will facilitate driving it in, especially when working with hardwood.

18. Of the following, the kind of head with which screws do NOT come is   18.____

    A. flat   B. round   C. oval   D. square

19. The one of the following lengths of screws which can be purchased is   19.____

    A. 1/8"   B. 3/16"   C. 5/16"   D. 3/8"

20. The one of the following lengths of screws which CANNOT be purchased is   20.____

    A. 1 1/8"   B. 1 1/2"   C. 1 1/2"   D. 13/4"

21. The one of the following lengths of screws which can be purchased is   21.____

    A. 3 3/4"   B. 4 1/2"   C. 4 2/4"   D. 4 3/4"

22. The type of screw used for countersinking is the one whose head is   22.____

    A. flat   B. round   C. oval   D. square

23. To facilitate driving a screw in, it should FIRST be   23.____
   A. countersunk   B. sanded
   C. soaped   D. varnished

24. The word *facilitate,* as used in the above paragraph, means MOST NEARLY to make   24.____
   A. angular   B. artificial   C. difficult   D. easy

Questions 25.

DIRECTIONS: Question 25 is based on the following statement.

Interior painting may be done at any time, provided that temperature can be kept above 50° F for ordinary paints and above 65° F for enamels and varnishes.

25. According to this statement, the temperature for enameling and varnishing should be   25.____
   A. above 50° F   B. between 50° F and 65° F
   C. below 65° F   D. above 65° F

KEY (CORRECT ANSWERS)

1. B	11. A
2. D	12. A
3. B	13. C
4. B	14. D
5. D	15. B
6. B	16. B
7. A	17. B
8. D	18. D
9. C	19. D
10. B	20. A

21. C
22. A
23. C
24. D
25. D

TEST 2

DIRECTIONS: Each question or incomplete statement is followed by several suggested answers or completions. Select the one that BEST answers the question or completes the statement. *PRINT THE LETTER OF THE CORRECT ANSWER IN THE SPACE AT THE RIGHT.* Questions 1 through 8 are based on the paragraphs below. Use only the information contained in these paragraphs in answering these questions.

Glue may be either hot or cold. Hot glue, an animal product, is purchased in dry flakes or sheets which must be soaked in water, then heated in a glue pot which is similar to a double boiler. Its main advantage is that it sets quickly, in fact so quickly that one must work fast to complete the joint before the glue sets.

There are numerous kinds of cold glue. One of the best is casein glue, which is manufactured from skimmed milk. It comes as a powder, which must be freshly mixed with water for each job, as the mixture will lose its valuable adhesive properties if stored. Cold glue is just as strong as hot glue, and casein glue resists moisture more effectively, but it needs considerable time to set.

1. The MAIN advantage of hot glue is that it   1.____

    A. is easily prepared
    B. is inexpensive
    C. resists moisture more effectively than cold glue
    D. sets quickly

2. Hot glue is purchased as   2.____

    A. dry flakes or sheets   B. a liquid
    C. a powder   D. wet film

3. Casein glue   3.____

    A. does not need to be mixed with water before application
    B. is purchased as a powder dissolved in water
    C. must be freshly mixed with water for each job
    D. should be mixed with water before storing away

4. The strength of cold glue in relation to that of hot glue is   4.____

    A. less
    B. the same
    C. greater
    D. variable, depending on type of glue

5. The time in which hot glue sets in relation to the time in which cold glue sets is 5.____

    A. shorter
    B. the same
    C. longer
    D. variable, depending on type of glue

6. If casein glue is mixed with water before storing, its adhesive strength will   6.____

   A. be lost
   B. remain the same
   C. increase
   D. increase or diminish, depending on amount of water used

7. Casein glue in relation to hot glue resists moisture   7.____

   A. less effectively
   B. about the same
   C. more effectively
   D. in varying degrees, depending on type of glue

8. The word *adhesive,* as used in the above paragraph, means MOST NEARLY   8.____

   A. costly   B. economical
   C. glowing brightly   D. sticking together

Questions 9-25.

DIRECTIONS: Each question consists of a statement. You are to indicate whether the statement is TRUE (T) or FALSE (F). *PRINT THE LETTER OF THE CORRECT ANSWER IN THE SPACE AT THE RIGHT.*

Questions 9-13.

DIRECTIONS: Questions 9 through 13, inclusive, are to be answered in accordance with the paragraph below.

Wood kept constantly dry or continuously submerged in water does not decay, regardless of species or the presence of sapwood. A large *proportion* of wood in use is kept so dry at all times that it lasts indefinitely. Moisture and temperature are the principal factors affecting the rate of decay. When exposed to conditions that favor decay, wood in warm humid areas of the United States deteriorates more rapidly than in cool or dry areas. High altitudes, as a rule, are less favorable to decay than are low altitudes because the *average* temperatures are lower and the growing season for fungi, which cause decay, are shorter.

9. A wooden beam is supporting a pier and is constantly under water. According to the   9.____
   above paragraph, the beam will have a high rate of decay.

10. According to the above paragraph, the cause of decay in wood is fungi.   10.____

11. According to the above paragraph, the LOWEST rate of decay in wood is found in cli-   11.____
    mates that are warm and humid.

12. As used in the above paragraph, *proportion* means MOST NEARLY *percent.*   12.____

13. As used in the above paragraph, *average* means MOST NEARLY *lowest.*   13.____

Questions 14-18.

DIRECTIONS: Questions 14 through 18, inclusive, are to be answered in accordance with the paragraph below.

HOW WOOD IS SEASONED

There are two common methods of drying lumber after it has been sawed. These two methods are air seasoning and kiln drying. Some woods may be air dried *satisfactorily* while others must be put through the kiln drying process before the wood can be successfully used for furniture-making. Most soft, non-porous woods are more easily air-dried than the harder woods. In the air drying process, the lumber is stacked carefully in large piles in the open air. Thin strips are laid between each layer of boards to prevent them from *warping* and to allow the air to circulate between them.

14.   According to the above paragraph, all wood can be dried by stacking the lumber in the open air.   14._____

15.   According to the above paragraph, if the wood in non-porous, it is better to air dry it.   15._____

16.   According to the above paragraph, drying of lumber is done after it is cut to size.   16._____

17.   As used in the above paragraph, the word *satisfactorily* means *quickly*.   17._____

18.   As used in the above paragraph, the word *warping* means *twisting*.   18._____

Questions 19-25.

DIRECTIONS: Questions 19 through 25, inclusive, are to be answered in accordance with the paragraph below.

CARE OF FURNITURE

Furniture, like floors, interior *trim,* and automobiles, requires frequent care to keep its finish in good condition. The finish of new furniture can be kept in good condition for many years if a coat of wax is *applied* to it regularly at least once each year. The coat of wax maintains the luster of the finish, protects the finishing coat from dampness, and aids in preventing the surface from being *marred* easily.

Excessive use of oil polishes should be avoided since they have a tendency to eventually produce a dull, lifeless surface and cause dust to collect on the finish.

If water has been allowed to remain on a finished surface for some time, it often causes the finish to turn white. The natural color of the finish may usually be restored by rubbing the spots lightly with a cloth moistened with alcohol, followed by the application of a small amount of sweet oil or linseed oil. Excessive moisture often collects on the furniture during the winter season as a result of improper ventilation and the use of open-flame gas stoves. This condition effects the joints and finish and causes the furniture to deteriorate rapidly.

A touch-up pencil may be obtained for the purpose of filling and removing deep scratches and other blemishes from a finished surface.

19. According to the above paragraph, one function of a coat of wax on furniture is to prevent penetration of moisture.   19._____

20. According to the above paragraph, water stains can be removed by FIRST applying a small amount of linseed oil.   20._____

21. According to the above paragraph, it is good practice to apply frequent coats of oil polish.   21._____

22. According to the above paragraph, one reason for the excess moisture that collects on furniture in the winter time is poor ventilation.   22._____

23. As used in the above paragraph, the word *trim* means *walls*.   23._____

24. As used in the above paragraph, the word *marred* means *damaged*.   24._____

25. As used in the above paragraph, the word *applied* means *rubbed*.   25._____

———

KEY (CORRECT ANSWERS)

1.	D		11.	F
2.	A		12.	T
3.	C		13.	F
4.	B		14.	F
5.	A		15.	F
6.	A		16.	T
7.	C		17.	F
8.	D		18.	T
9.	F		19.	T
10.	T		20.	F

21.	F
22.	T
23.	F
24.	T
25.	F

———

TEST 3

DIRECTIONS: Each question consists of a statement. You are to indicate whether the statement is TRUE (T) or FALSE (F). *PRINT THE LETTER OF THE CORRECT ANSWER IN THE SPACE AT THE RIGHT.*

Questions 1 -7.

DIRECTIONS: Questions 1 through 7, inclusive, are to be answered in accordance with the paragraph below.

There are several types of lines in a blueprint. The solid line that represents edges of surfaces are somewhat heavier than the other lines on the drawing and are known as working lines. These lines may be straight or curved, depending upon the shape and view of the object. Dotted lines are the same as working lines, except that the surface which is represented by dotted lines is hidden from sight when the object is viewed. To show the size of any structure, or part of it, dimension lines are used. These lines are light lines drawn between two working lines to show the dimensions between two points. If the dimension lines cannot readily be placed on view, the working lines are lengthened or extended in order that the dimension lines may be drawn. These lines are known as extension lines. A shaded area of a drawing made by a series of parallel lines drawn close together at any angle to the working lines of the view is sometimes found on a blueprint. These are known as section lines. They represent what would be seen if that part of the view covered by such lines were cut through and a portion removed.

1. The number of different types of blueprint lines described in the above paragraph is 4. 1.____

2. According to the above paragraph, the HEAVIEST lines on a blueprint are usually the working lines. 2.____

3. According to the above paragraph, extension lines are continuations of working lines 3.____

4. The following line appears on a blueprint 6'4". According to the above paragraph, this line is BEST described as a dimension line. 4.____

5. According to the above paragraph, the shaded area of a blueprint represents what would be seen if that part of the view were cut through and a portion removed. 5.____

6. According to the above paragraph, dimension lines may appear between two section lines. 6.____

7. According to the above paragraph, a series of parallel lines drawn close together at an angle to the working lines are the dotted lines. 7.____

Questions 8-14.

DIRECTIONS: Questions 8 through 14, inclusive, are to be answered in accordance with the paragraph below.

Native species of trees are divided into two *classes*-hardwoods, which have broad leaves, and softwoods, which have scalelike leaves, as the cedars, or needlelike leaves, as the pines. Hardwoods, except in the warmest regions, shed their leaves at the end of each growing season. Native softwoods, except cypress, tamarack and larch, are evergreen. The terms *hardwood* and *softwood* have no direct application to the hardness or softness of the wood. In fact, such hardwood trees as cottonwood and aspen have softer wood than the white pines and true firs, and *certain* softwoods, such as longleaf pine and Douglas-fir, produce wood that is as hard as that of basswood and yellow-poplar.

8. According to the above paragraph, softwoods are differentiated from hardwoods by the types of leaves.
8.____

9. According to the above paragraph, if a tree sheds its leaves in the winter, you can be sure it is a hardwood.
9.____

10. According to the above paragraph, an example of a tree that stays green throughout the year is cypress.
10.____

11. According to the above paragraph, hardwoods are NOT necessarily *harder* than softwoods.
11.____

12. According to the above paragraph, one of the *harder* softwoods is basswood.
12.____

13. As used in the above paragraph, *classes* means *groups.*
13.____

14. As used in the above paragraph, *certain* means *sure.*
14.

Questions 15-20.

DIRECTIONS: Questions 15 through 20, inclusive, are to be answered in accordance with the paragraph below.

Sometimes it is impossible to scrape and sand out all blemishes and defects in the wood surfaces. Nail holes left where nailheads have been set below the surface, dents, checks, and pits caused by faulty grain, especially in cedar, usually cannot be removed from the surface. It, therefore, is necessary to fill these defects with a special filler. Some of the better types of fillers used for this purpose include colored stick shellac, plastic wood, and various *types* of crack fillers. It is especially important to use a filler that will match the color of the wood when it is finished. It is *usually* best to stain a scrap piece of wood with the stain that is to be used on the finished project and match the color of the filler to it. Stick shellac and plastic wood may be obtained in various colors, but these colors cannot be changed satisfactorily. Crack fillers may be obtained in various colors and may also be colored to match the color of the stain being used.

15. According to the above paragraph, one of the defects often found in wood is knots.
15.____

16. According to the above paragraph, the BEST method of insuring good color match is to first test the color on a piece of scrap wood.
16.____

17. According to the above paragraph, the one of the types of fillers whose color can be changed is *crack filler.*
17.____

18. According to the above paragraph, it is fairly easy to remove defects from the surface of the wood.
18.____

19. As used in the above paragraph, the word *usually* means *frequently.*
19.____

20. As used in the above paragraph, the word *types* means *kinds*.

20.____

Questions 21-25.

DIRECTIONS: Questions 21 through 25, inclusive, are to be answered in accordance with the paragraph below.

By *squaring stock* is meant the process of working all the surfaces of the stock until they have been made smooth and true, until they are at right angles to the adjoining surfaces, and until opposite surfaces are *parallel* to each other. The quality of your finished project will be determined largely by your ability to square stock quickly and accurately. The *process* of squaring stock is the fundamental basis of all woodworking. Each part of the piece should be accurately squared to *dimensions* in order to insure a proper fit when joined with the other parts of the project.

21. According to the above paragraph, one of the reasons for squaring stock is so that the pieces will fit properly when joined.

21.____

22. According to the above paragraph, the quality of the work will depend upon how accurately you can square.

22.____

23. As used in the above paragraph, the word *parallel* means *at right angles*.

23.____

24. As used in the above paragraph, the word *process* means *ability*.

24.____

25. As used in the above paragraph, the word *dimensions* means *sizes*

25.____

KEY (CORRECT ANSWERS)

1. F		11. T	
2. T		12. F	
3. T		13. T	
4. T		14. F	
5. T		15. F	
6. F		16. T	
7. F		17. T	
8. T		18. F	
9. F		19. F	
10. F		20. T	

21. T
22. T
23. F
24. F
25. T

CONCISE TEXT

THE FOREMAN

BASIC FUNDAMENTALS OF SUPERVISION AND MANAGEMENT

CONTENTS

THE FOREMAN

Basic Fundamentals of Supervision and Management

I. The Job of the Foreman

- ❖ His duties and responsibilities
- ❖ His authority
- ❖ Special problems of the foreman in a small plant.

A foreman is the member of plant management who has been delegated the authority to manage a shop, a function, or a department. He is the one whom the folks in the shop call boss; he is the one they look to for instructions and supervision; and he shoulders the responsibility for all work done by those who report to him. In short, he is the first line of management. In this position he is a key figure both as a production manager and in the plant's relationships with its employees.

His duties and responsibilities

The foreman's job is to use the men, machines, and material assigned to him, for the purpose of getting out production under conditions specified by his superiors. In order to accomplish this objective, he has to perform a multitude of duties and responsibilities.

Human relations duties:

1. To maintain good relationships with employees, with other departments in the plant, with his superiors, with customers, with unions, and with the public.
2. To settle grievances—one of his most important duties.
3. To be familiar with the union contract if there is one, and to run the shop in strict accordance with it.
4. To be familiar with company policies and interpret them to the workers as management has explained them to him.
5. To exercise leadership and supervision over the people assigned to him.
6. To develop and maintain job interest among his employees.
7. To be available when those who report to him need help or assistance, whether it be of a business or personal nature.

Training duties:

1. To inform new employees assigned to him about company policies.
2. To see that new employees receive adequate job instruction.
3. To train an understudy who can take his place in the event he is absent, or is promoted, or resigns.

Production duties:

1. *Schedules*—He is expected to get the production out in accordance with schedules prescribed by his superiors; to coordinate the various activities in his department for the purpose of eliminating delays and bottlenecks; and to see that the men, materials, and

machines assigned to him are fully utilized.

2. *Quality*— He is expected to protect the customer from the receipt of faulty products through proper shop precautions.
3. *Costs*— He is expected to keep production costs within the budget approved by his superiors.
4. *General production duties*— He is expected to be constantly alert to new methods and procedures which will improve quality, reduce delays, and reduce production costs; he is also expected to see that all production activities conform with plant safety regulations.

Although the duties of a foreman vary by necessity from plant to plant, the ones listed above cover the basic responsibilities which most foremen are expected to shoulder.

His authority

A foreman's authority to make decisions and take action is delegated to him by his superiors. While this, too, must of necessity vary according to the circumstances, most foremen have the following general types of authority.

Supervision.—This involves the authority to exercise full supervision over the men, materials, machines, and supplies assigned to his department- within the limits of company policies.

Use of productive facilities.—This involves the authority to requisition materials, supplies and personnel and incur certain other expenses within the limits of his approved budget.

Maintenance of quality— This involves the authority to reject any item produced in his shop which fails in his opinion to meet standards of quality as prescribed by his superiors.

Control of jobs.—This involves, for some foremen, the authority to hire and fire.

A foreman's influence is often greater than his specific authority. In certain areas, his superior may regard him as a personal representative, and by virtue of that fact, the foreman's recommendations carry considerable weight. For example, his recommendations concerning personnel, product design, the need for more shop space, new production processes or formulas, and new equipment are given careful consideration. He is usually closer to problems of this nature than any other official in the plant. In the eyes of the workers, the foreman's authority within the shop is all inclusive. If by chance the workers have any question on this score, it is only because the foreman's superiors fail to back him up adequately.

In exercising his authority, and in accepting responsibilities, the foreman acts as a member of a team the management team. But as in any kind of team work, he must also rely upon his superiors for advice, guidance, and information. Likewise, his superiors are dependent on him for information and suggestions. Crystallizing this concept of teamwork in the minds of all members of management is perhaps the greatest single element of help that can be given to foremen. It encourages greater cooperation between the foreman's shop and other departments, and as a result, the whole company benefits from it. In addition, the foreman needs the cooperation and support of every department with which he comes in contact if he is to do his job effectively.

Special problems of the foreman in a small plant

The problems of a foreman in a small plant are often different from those of a foreman in a large company. There are two basic reasons why this is true:

First, small plants can't always afford the services of those specialized departments which are accepted as an essential part of the organization in a large plant. For example, relatively few small plants enjoy the benefit of time-study specialists, of full-time production inspectors, or of separate machine maintenance departments. Although such services may not be handled by specialized personnel, the work still has to be done, and quite often the responsibility for doing it is assigned to the foreman. As a result, the duties and problems of small-plant foremen are usually broader in scope than are those of foremen in a larger plant.

Second, a small plant typically operates on a more intimate basis than a large one. Thus, the relationships between department heads are more personal, and as a result everybody gets to know everybody else much better than is possible in a larger plant. Similarly, department heads are more dependent upon each other for cooperation and help. In such a situation, the foreman has to be doubly alert to the value of good personal relationships, because one unfortunate experience with just one department head in the plant can create a problem between himself and the heads of several other departments. If such an incident occurs, and it results in less cooperation between his shop and other departments, his value to the company is greatly diminished. For this reason the foreman must be an accepted member of the small plant family, in fact as well as theory, or else he has no place in the organization. Therefore, the smaller the plant, the more important personal relationships become.

II. Basic Responsibilities of a Foreman

- ❖ **Getting production out on time**
- ❖ **Maintaining quality standards**
- ❖ **Holding production costs down**
- ❖ **How top management can help foremen improve efficiency.**

The foreman has three basic responsibilities:

1. Getting production out on time.
2. Getting production to conform with quality standards.
3. Getting production out at the least possible cost

Unless a foreman can satisfy these three responsibilities, he is unable to live up to the requirements of his job.

Getting production out on time

The foreman's department has to satisfy certain production quotas because customers want to receive their purchases within a certain period of time. In order to make sure that customers get their shipments within the time specified, one of the foreman's superiors usually develops a production schedule in consultation with the foreman, the sales department, and other interested departments. This schedule then becomes a timetable to which operations must be geared. It places a maximum limit on the amount of time that can be allowed to produce a given number of units. The foreman's objective, insofar as schedules are concerned, should not only be to get production out on schedule, but to get it put as much ahead of schedule as possible, within the resources of his department.

In meeting schedule deadlines, a foreman needs to maintain a set of figures which will tell him at the end of each day how his shop is producing. These figures should tell him that the shop is either adequately or inadequately organized for getting the work out on time. Without such information, his ability to meet schedules is left up to chance.

For example, if a schedule calls for the production of 220 units in a 30-day month, the foreman knows that his shop has 22 work days in which to do the job required. When, during any given day, less than 10 units are produced, he knows he is falling behind schedule and can take remedial action before the production deadline arrives. The foreman's superiors are also interested in these figures and he has a responsibility to keep them posted at all times as to the progress in relation to the scheduled requirements.

Sometimes production falls behind schedule for reasons which have to be referred to higher authority for correction. For example, shipments of raw materials which are needed to produce the finished product may be delayed by the supplier; abnormal sickness may require overtime by others and approval to thus add to expenses; or a machine may break down and delay production to such an extent that the schedule has to be revised.

However, most of the reasons for a shop falling behind schedule are due to internal conditions. Ingenuity of the foreman in identifying the causes and taking remedial action is a test of his ability to hold down the job of foreman. Some of the most common conditions which lie within the authority of the foreman to correct are as follows:

Materials.—The material which goes into the production process may be located in an inconvenient spot. It may be placed where it is so inaccessible or located so far away from the workers that much valuable production time is lost in transporting the material to the machines.

Frequently a more efficient arrangement of materials will solve the production lag problem. The foreman has to be alert to the need for having raw materials placed in the best location.

Schedule balance.—Oftentimes the workers engaged in producing a certain part of the product will get ahead of those who are producing other parts. This leaves workers who turn out the finished items standing idle until the parts from the lagging operations shop are available. Since all parts of a given product must be produced on schedule, if the deadline for completed units is to be met, the foreman often has to redistribute the number of men and machines assigned to a given phase of the operation in order to maintain the proper balance of output between the various operations being performed.

Work simplification.—Sometimes the number of operations performed by each worker are so great or so unrelated that the rate of production is slowed down. In such a case production can be speeded up if the job of each worker is broken down so that he has a smaller variety of steps to perform. Frequently, depending upon the nature of the product being produced, this saves time because it reduces the motions in changing from one operation to another. This is a possibility the foreman has to consider, for often it is the key to quicker production.

Machine utilization.—Scheduling the work in proper sequence and with balanced timing is essential if the foreman expects to get maximum use out of each available machine. Regular inspection and maintenance of each machine is also essential if disruptive breakdowns are to be avoided. Down time is expensive: it adds to production costs, to say nothing of the cost of the investment in equipment.

Worker utilization.—Placing workers on those phases of the operation where they can do most effective work is also an aid to meeting production schedules' The foreman has to know how much work each employee is producing, and how his production compares with those around him in order that the slow ones may be singled out for consultation. A worker who is a laggard on one job may do better work on other jobs for which he is better adapted.

In order to meet production requirements, a foreman must maintain a delicate balance between the men, the machines and the materials in his shop. Failure to maintain the balance will result in disrupted production and eventual failure to meet the scheduled deadline.

Maintaining quality standards

Production has to conform with quality standards as prescribed by top management because the customer will return any unit which fails to meet those standards. If such returns reach significant proportions, the reputation and prestige of the plant suffers. Because of the embarrassment arising from the sale of faulty goods to customers, most plants have an arrangement whereby finished goods are inspected before they are shipped to the customer. If, upon inspection, it is found that the product meets all quality standards, it is approved for shipment. If it doesn't, it is rejected and sent back to the shop for more attention. The practice of conducting such inspections is commonly referred to as "quality control." Some plants, especially those which produce critical items (such as parachutes), inspect every unit before it is "o. k.'d." But this is expensive, and hence other plants use a type of statistical quality control. This is a system whereby only one unit out of a given number of units is checked, with the assumption that if the units checked are found all right, then those in between are likewise all right. The system is becoming more popular in plants and is proving to be effective.

The ideal arrangement is to have finished production inspected by someone who reports to the foreman's superior. This is desirable because the inspector is checking work which the foreman is responsible for producing, and a person who has no responsibility to the foreman, or who has had no part in the production of the items can usually be more objective in his inspections. However, in some of the smaller plants, when inspectors are not carried on the payroll, the inspection function may be delegated to the foreman himself.

Under either arrangement, the foreman should maintain the following information concerning units which are rejected, for use in improving the quality of production:

1. The number of units rejected within the plant each day, week, or month (whichever is most practicable);
2. The number of units rejected by customers each day, week, or month;
3. The name of the worker who produced the unit, if such information is available.

The inspector should keep both the foreman and his superiors advised of the number of units rejected by him. The foreman's superiors should keep the foreman and the inspector advised regarding the number of units rejected by the customers. These records should be used by all three parties to determine whether the number of rejections is excessive. If the number of units rejected exceeds the average rate, it is then up to the foreman to check with the employees responsible and reanalyze his procedures to determine what corrective action is necessary. However, even though the number of rejections is below normal, the foreman still has a responsibility to devise ways and means of effecting further reductions. *The best foremen have the lowest rejection rates.*

Holding production costs down

The use of shop budgets for cost control purposes is the most effective means for making the foreman cost conscious. This is true because he knows that he either has to live within his budget or explain the reasons why. In many plants, the cost accountant prepares a monthly report showing detailed types of expenses as charged to each department in relation to the amount budgeted. This report is useful to top management because it tells how effectively the foreman has controlled his expenses during the previous month. It also serves as a useful supervisory tool for the foreman because it tells him what particular expenditures exceeded the budget, which enables him to know in which area remedial action is necessary.

However, if the foreman is to operate his department as effectively as possible, he can't wait until the end of the month to see how good its performance has been. He usually needs to know on the following day how well he did the day before; in other words, he needs daily expense figures which he can compare with daily budget figures. Such figures on a rounded basis can be easily developed by the foreman himself. All he needs to do is take the previous month's budget report and develop from it average daily budget figures which will give him a fairly good idea of what his maximum daily expenses for the current month should be. He can then develop an estimate on the following day which will tell him what his approximate costs were on the previous day. By comparing the previous day's estimates with his estimated daily expense budget he can get a fairly good idea of how well his expenses are being controlled. If accurate daily performance records can be developed, they of course are more desirable than estimated figures. But many small plants do not have the resources for keeping detailed expense records on a daily basis.

The budget covering the foreman's shop should be prepared by the foreman himself. This not only accentuates the importance of the foreman's responsibility, but it is a more realistic way of preparing a budget. The foreman is closer to the needs of his department than anyone else and if the budget is prepared by someone farther removed from the shop activities, it cannot be all-inclusive and will usually result in the foreman asking for authority to exceed the budget because something was overlooked when it was originally set up. If, after the foreman prepares the budget, his superiors want to cut some of the estimated costs, they then have a more realistic set of figures from which they can estimate what adjustments should be made.

Once a foreman's budget has been established, he should clearly understand that he is expected to keep his expenditures within budgetary limitations. Authority to exceed the budgeted amount should be granted only upon the specific request of the foreman, and only after it has been determined how far he should exceed the budget and for what type of expenditure.

A good foreman not only wants to keep within his budget, he wants to keep his expenditures as far below the budget as possible because he wants to be a good enough administrator to get the production out with the least possible cost.

A budget report to be effectively used as a means of controlling expenditures in the shop, should be issued in final form by the accounting people once a month. It should show both the actual and budgeted monthly expense for the following items:

1. Direct labor costs.
2. Indirect labor costs.
3. Material costs.
4. Maintenance costs.
5. Costs of supplies, including tools.
6. Light, heat, power, and telephone costs.

These are controllable costs (some, of course, are more controllable than others) which the foreman should be conscious of at all times. Other items of a non-controllable nature are also usually included in the budget report. However, as long as the foreman gets reports covering his controllable expenses, he has something which he can use to guide him hi his efforts to run a more efficient shop.

The foreman has to be continually conscious of the cost which results from everything that goes on in the shop. Here is a list of some of the major areas on which a foreman has to keep a particularly watchful eye if he is to successfully hold expenses down:

Direct labor costs.—You don't normally cut costs by cuffing wages because lower wages attract less efficient people and in the long run, a wage cut often increases labor costs. In fact, some shops have been known to cut costs by raising wages, because through higher wages they were able to attract more efficient people. As a result, less people were needed to turn out the production. The real personnel costs that can and must be controlled are those resulting from absenteeism, turnover, accidents, and improper utilization of workers.

A worker who is guilty of excessive absenteeism increases shop costs because the work schedule of the shop has to be readjusted each time he is absent. That costs money. This is a matter which should be ironed out on a personal basis between the employee and the foreman on the merits of each case.

Excessive turnover is also costly. It is costly in terms of the time and effort used (1) to find and process replacements; (2) to train new employees to your equipment and your methods. Furthermore, it is costly in terms of productivity: it is usually several weeks or longer before the performance of new employees equals that of your experienced workers. The problem of excessive turnover can, in many cases, be clarified by getting from each employee the reasons for his leaving. Both the foreman and the personnel department should be interested in such information. Once the true reasons for turnover are known, corrective action can be taken. High turnover is frequently caused by poor selection, low wages, or poor supervision on the part of the foreman.

When a worker is incapacitated because of an occupational accident, not only does the company temporarily lose his services, but hospital bills, increased workmen's compensation assessments, increased insurance rates, and law suits are apt to result. While not all of these charges would be reflected in the foreman's budget, nevertheless hospital charges and other miscellaneous items become a part of his labor costs.

Failure by the foreman to utilize fully the time an employee is on the job results in increased production costs not only because the worker is being paid for time he has not worked, but because failure to use the regular man-hours available may force the foreman to resort to overtime work in order to get production out on time. A foreman should organize the next day's work before he leaves the shop at night. This is the best way to assure full utilization of all employees.

Indirect labor costs.—These are the labor costs which have nothing to do with actual manufacturing or production costs, such as the cost of labor required sweeping the floors, and repairing the machines. In order to keep indirect labor costs to a minimum, the foreman will do well to keep his eye on two major items: the cost of maintaining machines and the cost of handling raw materials. In small plants especially, responsibility for the costs of these functions falls upon the production foreman.

Experience proves that it is cheaper to inspect machines at regular intervals and replace worn parts than to wait until they break down. For when a machine breaks down, its repair usually costs more than keeping the machine in good condition through the process of regular inspection. In addition, a broken-down machine disrupts production, which results in even greater expense.

Perhaps one of the most overlooked expense items in the indirect labor category is the cost of materials handling. It has been estimated, for example, that 36 percent of the labor dollar in the electrical industry is spent in moving materials destined to go into the production process from one place to another. When the material arrives at the plant, it is moved into the warehouse. While there it may be moved several times to make room for other incoming shipments. Then it is moved to the shop, where it may be moved again several times before it is finally used in production. Such a procedure not only makes indirect labor costs excessively high, but also increases the cost of material because the more the material is moved, the more it is in danger of being damaged.

Material utilization.—The foreman can cut the cost of materials by developing standardized procedures for employees to follow in cutting up a piece of material. Most pieces come in standard sizes and lend themselves to formal cutting procedures which can result in considerable savings. A furniture factory, for instance, has found that a piece of plywood which comes in standard 4x8 foot sizes can make a small bookcase with only one-half of a board foot to spare, if the cutting is done in a certain way. If the piece is cut any other way, it takes two such pieces, with a lot of material left over. Most of it cannot be used at all, and the part that is usable can be used only by disrupting the assembly line. Material costs are a big factor in production and proper utilization can help hold production costs down.

Machine utilization.—Machines cost money whether they are utilized or not because they depreciate and become obsolete. To justify these costs, machines should be fully utilized at all times through proper work organization. Therefore, before the foreman goes home at night, he should know exactly how every employee and machine will be utilized when the shop opens up the next day.

Methods improvement.—To do his job of keeping costs down to a minimum, a foreman must be, in addition to everything else, an "efficiency expert." He must constantly be on the lookout for better, cheaper, and easier ways of getting the production out. He should consider such things as the number of steps a worker must take in going from one operation to another; a rearrangement of equipment will save money if that will cut down on the number of steps required. He needs to consider the number of motions a worker must go through to complete a given operation; if a change in procedure will make some motions unnecessary, he has saved the company money.

In attempting to make his shop as efficient as possible, the foreman can make progress if he will look to his employees for ideas. They are in a position to see many things which he is either unable or too busy to see. Some of the best ideas for increasing efficiency in plants come from employees. A formalized suggestion plan promoted by the foremen will serve as a stimulus for employees to develop new ideas and turn them in. A suggestion plan if properly promoted can be one of the most effective steps toward greater plant efficiency.

How top management can help foremen improve efficiency

There are at least three things which top management can do which will help the foreman improve the efficiency of his shop:

Let him have a voice in the purchase of materials, tools and equipment.—The foreman lives every day with the materials, tools and equipment in his department. He knows the good and bad points of every brand-name in his shop. He knows which items speed up production and which ones do not. While there is no need to give the foreman the last word on purchases made for his shop, he should be given the opportunity to express his opinions on the matter. In most cases, he will be able to offer ideas that will influence the type of purchases to be made. This should result in having more efficient equipment and in improved morale of the work force.

Let him select his own employees.—Recruiting of personnel should be done through the personnel office, based upon qualifications submitted by the foreman. But the foreman should have the authority to determine which of the applicants submitted by the personnel office he wants to have in his department. This enables the foreman to select those people whom he feels will be most capable of doing the job the way he wants it done. Such an arrangement is conducive to a more harmonious shop, and helps give the foreman the prestige necessary to carry out his responsibility. The personnel office should continue to make personnel policies to which the foreman should of course conform, but a foreman should have the freedom to select his own employees within the limits of those policies.

Give the foreman authority to recommend or deny wage increases.—If the foreman wants to have the wages of one of his employees raised, he should have the authority to recommend the increase. Moreover, every effort should be made to grant it, provided it does not conflict with the plant's overall personnel policies. This procedure helps also to increase the prestige of the foreman and gives the workers assurance that their ability to get wage increases is not dependent solely upon some higher authority who is unfamiliar with their work. Conversely, if the worker's performance does not, in the opinion of the foreman, justify a proposed wage increase, he should be authorized to deny it. If the plant is a union shop, of course, suitable adjustments in these policies would have to be made.

III. The Foreman's Training Functions

- ❖ **Training new employees**
- ❖ **Training employees promoted to new jobs**
- ❖ **Training an understudy-Other training responsibilities.**

A foreman has to assume certain training functions— whether the plant has a training department or not because there are certain procedures and techniques which are peculiar to many jobs. In a small plant, it is often difficult for anyone outside of the department in question to be entirely familiar with its procedures and techniques. Moreover, procedural changes often take place so fast that a centralized training department would find it almost impossible to keep on a current basis.

Training new employees

The foreman has a threefold training responsibility for new employees:

Explaining company policies.—He has a responsibility, at the time the new employee reports for work, to brief him on all company policies which directly relate to him individually; for example: regulations regarding pay, including lost time and overtime, seniority provisions, seniority increases, union contract provisions, and promotions; company-sponsored insurance plans; workmen's compensation, and the rights of the employee in connection with each. These are items of such importance to the new employee that they are an essential part of his orientation.

Instruction covering shop operations.—The foreman also has a responsibility to introduce the new employee around the shop, explain the functions of each worker, point out the different types of equipment and what they are used for, and explain shop safety regulations. He also should explain the relationship of the new employee's job to the rest of the department and to the rest of the company, and briefly outline the organization of the company as a whole. This helps the employee to get a proper perspective of his new job and the plant.

Coaching covering the job of a new employee.—The foreman has a responsibility to see that the new employee is properly broken in on his new job. This is usually done by assigning him to an experienced employee who provides detailed instruction and assistance until the new worker is qualified to handle his assignments alone.

When a new employee is hired for a complicated job requiring several different types of operations, foremen frequently break the job down into a series of simple steps, to facilitate training. When the new employee learns how to handle the first operation, he is then instructed on how to do the second operation until he has mastered that step, and so on. This is known as the "job dilution" type of training. It was widely used in shops both large and small during World War II. This method of breaking in a new employee on a complicated job usually accelerates the training period with a minimum of effort.

Training employees promoted to new jobs

When an employee is promoted or transferred to a different job, the foreman has a responsibility to see that adequate instruction is given the worker on his new job until he is qualified to handle his assignments alone. As in the case of a newly hired employee, such training usually requires that an experienced employee provide the necessary detailed instruction.

Training an understudy

The foreman has a responsibility to develop an understudy who can take over his job if and when he is promoted or leaves the company.

Some men hesitate to develop an understudy because they feel he may eventually prove to be a competitor for the job of foreman. Yet a foreman owes it to himself to have an understudy who can take his place. Failure to have one may prevent him from being promoted to a better job, simply because there is no one to take his place. In many cases, an oversight of this nature has stood in the way of a foreman's promotion.

From the plant manager's viewpoint, an understudy is desirable because of the possibility that the foreman may get sick, leave the company, or be eligible for transfer or promotion.

Other training responsibilities

Foremen are often given other types of training responsibilities, among which are the following:

Orientation of salesmen and other company personnel.—Foremen are often called upon to explain the production process to salesmen for their information in selling the product to customers. Others in the company who hold management positions often call upon the foreman to give them the same briefing so they can get a more complete picture of plant operations. Sometimes foremen are called upon to explain the production process to customers who want to know how the product they buy is made.

Special training sessions for employees.—When major changes are made in the production process; plant mechanization is increased; wage payment systems are changed; time-study plans are introduced; plant operations are reorganized, or special sales and advertising campaigns are initiated, the foreman has a responsibility to explain to his employees the reasons why the changes are taking place, and how these changes will affect them.

Some plants, realizing that the foreman is the company so far as his employees are concerned, rely upon him to hold employee training sessions in cooperation with other supervisors for the purpose of acquainting employees with the operations of the company in general, why it operates the way it does, what the plant balance sheet shows, what the current business conditions are and how they affect the operations of the company, and what the prospects of the company are for the future. Such sessions help to educate the worker with respect to economics and the free enterprise system. Most research organizations agree that employees are in need of such training because many of them are often ill-informed on matters of this nature.

IV. The Foreman's Personal Relationships and Contacts

- ❖ **Relationships with workers**
- ❖ **Contacts with supervisors in other departments**
- ❖ **Relationships with superiors**
- ❖ **Contacts with unions and union officials**
- ❖ **Contacts with the public.**

In the average small plant, each function and each department is so interdependent that the foreman who succeeds in establishing good personal relationships throughout the company has a much easier time performing his job. Since the foreman's shop is dependent upon other departments for materials, equipment, supplies, and personnel, the amount of cooperation he is able to get from other departments has a definite effect upon the performance of his shop.

Relationships with workers

The value of good personal relationships between the foreman and his employees cannot be overestimated, because it is through such good relationships that he is able to settle more grievances and avert more union complaints than any other member of the management team. A foreman in one small plant, for example, is known to have settled an average of one grievance a month for the past 5 years. His technique is simple. He listens until the worker gets the complaint off his chest. Then, if the worker is upset at the time the complaint is made, he waits until the next day, when the subject can be discussed more objectively. If after investigation, he finds that the complaint is valid, he takes corrective action-provided his department is at fault. If another department is at fault, such as the payroll or personnel office, he requests the department in question to take corrective action. And he follows up on the matter until the case is closed.

If a foreman does not enjoy good personal relationships with his employees, they may not choose to discuss their grievances with him. They may, instead, take them direct to the union and thereby strain the relationship between union and plant before the matter is settled. There is evidence that good foreman-employee relationships have been responsible for smoothing out many grievances which otherwise would have resulted in strikes.

Foremen who enjoy the best personal relationships with their employees are those whose actions prove that they sincerely have the interest of their workers at heart. Such action becomes evident in the foreman's efforts to provide his employees with adequate equipment and supplies; when he tries to make the job easier for them; when he tries to improve their comfort while on the job; when he takes an interest in seeing that they get their pay checks on time and in the right amount; when he makes allowances for illness in the family or other personal difficulties of his workers; and when he tries to promote harmony among all of the people in his department.

Many foremen find that occasional parties after work help to improve morale by enabling everybody to get acquainted. Also, occasional social visits to the homes of his employees improves their job interest and enables the foreman to know them better. If a foreman operates his shop on a strictly impartial basis, visits to the homes of his employees are a great help in improving morale.

Contacts with supervisors in other departments

Much that is used within a shop, such as materials and supplies, comes from other departments. The foreman therefore has to have the cooperation of these other departments if he is to get from them the kind of service he needs in order to keep his shop running efficiently.

While it is true that he can appeal to his superior if the cooperation he wants from other departments is not adequate, this procedure takes time. It creates even worse feelings, and in the long run, the foreman who made the complaint loses more than he gains. There is no substitute for good, spontaneous, interdepartmental cooperation.

Relationships with superiors

The foreman has a responsibility to keep his superiors informed regarding his problems, his needs and the overall operations of his department. Top management relies on information of this nature for control and planning purposes. He also has a responsibility to keep his superiors currently informed regarding those problems and situations affecting the performance of his shop which are outside the scope of his authority to handle. Failure to keep his superiors properly informed may result in eventual embarrassment to the foreman because a small problem, over which he has no control, may later develop into a major problem if it is allowed to go unattended.

Contacts with unions and union officials

A foreman's contacts with unions and union officials must at all times be honest and sincere. There is no other way to deal effectively with unions. It is a foreman's responsibility to respect and abide by the agreement which his company and his employees' union have developed. The foreman helps to promote better management-labor relations when the union knows that he fully respects and makes a sincere effort to support all provisions of the agreement which his company has signed.

Contacts with the public

The foreman is often called upon to handle plant tours for groups who want to see how products are manufactured. This places a public relations responsibility upon the foreman to give such visitors a good impression of the plant. Industrial management is becoming more and more aware of the need to acquaint the general public with the facts about its plants and the contributions which they make to the community. One of the more effective ways to do this is through plant tours.

The heads of many plants encourage the foremen and other supervisors to take part as much as possible in civic activities designed to improve the community in which the plant is located. They take the position that since the plant is a part of the community, the leadership in that plant should take a definite interest in community affairs. When the foreman engages in such activities, he not only advertises his company as being a civic-minded organization, but he assumes community responsibilities which contribute to the growth of both himself and the community.

V. Developing Better Foremen

- ❖ **Qualifications which foremen need**
- ❖ **Finding prospects**
- ❖ **What kind of training?**
- ❖ **Solving the problem in small plants**
- ❖ **Measuring the results**
- ❖ **How top management promotes foreman development.**

The problem of developing better foremen is more than just a matter of putting them through a foremanship training course. In fact, a training program is only one of several factors which have a bearing on the development of foremen. Before there can be effective training, it must first be determined that the foremen and prospective foremen possess the basic qualifications which such a job demands. Any time spent in training people in foremanship is wasted unless those being trained actually have the qualifications necessary to absorb and use such training effectively.

Even then, the maximum effectiveness of a foreman training program cannot be realized unless top management follows up such training with an arrangement which provides proper recognition of the role which a foreman is expected to play in his organization. If a foreman completes a training course which stresses the importance of his job (and virtually all foremen training courses do stress this) and later finds that the importance of that job is minimized through lack of proper authority and recognition, part of the value of the training course is lost.

The problem of developing better foremen is therefore, one which involves three basic considerations: (1) the prospective foreman must be qualified for the job, (2) special training for development on the job should be available, and (3) the importance of the role the foreman is expected to play in the operation of the plant should be fully recognized.

Qualifications which foremen need

The wide publicity given in recent years to the importance of the role played by foremen in industry has developed a realization by top management that, in the eyes of the worker, the foreman is the company, and, in the eyes of the community, the company is judged in part by the impression the foreman makes on the general public. This realization has resulted in a more careful selection of people who are placed in such jobs. Since the foreman is charged with the responsibility of getting the job done in the quickest possible time and with the least possible expense, he must be a highly qualified person. Recent studies by management associations and research organizations generally indicate that top management today is booking for the following nine qualifications in the people who are considered for the position of foreman:

1. *Leadership ability*—A recent survey taken among 300 companies indicates that leadership ability is the first qualification that top management looks for in a prospective foreman. The modern concept of a foreman is one who provides leadership, not one who simply gives orders. His ability to get production out on time with the least possible cost is dependent to a large extent upon how effectively his leadership can stimulate job interest and satisfaction on

the part of his employees. A foreman is a good leader when his employees turn out a good job not because they have to but because they as employees want to do a good job.

2. *Organizing ability*—A foreman has men, machines, and materials assigned to him. He must have the ability to organize all three factors in an orderly, clear-cut, and simplified manner, whenever circumstances demand it. Nothing will break down the morale of a shop quicker than a situation where the work is so poorly organized that the employees are, figuratively, stepping on each other, or where some employees are overworked while others are standing around waiting for work. Unless a foreman has the administrative skill necessary to organize the work of his shop in a manner that will hold bottlenecks and trouble spots to a minimum, his other qualifications as a foreman will be of little value.

3. *Character.*—A foreman has to be honest and fair with his employees at all times. In this respect his reputation must be above reproach. One of the costliest operators a company can have is a foreman or supervisor who arouses suspicion and distrust. Employees will invariably produce less work under such supervision. Their morale will not only be low, but they will spend valuable production time worrying about what the foreman is going to do next. These results in rumors and secret discussions between employees on company time, which increases the time and the cost required to get out production.

4. *Judgment.*—Employees do better work when they have confidence in the foreman's judgment. Especially is this true in a shop where poor judgment could result in accidents to employees. Very often employees are asked to do a job or follow a procedure in which they do not see any merit. Confidence in the judgment of the foreman will tend to allay any fears that the foreman doesn't know what he is doing.

5. *Technical skill and mechanical ability*—The ideal foreman should be able to run any machine in the shop as well if not better than any employee under his supervision. It helps/strengthen his position as a leader. However, this is not always possible because some machines cannot be operated at peak efficiency unless a person has daily experience with them. Nevertheless, a foreman should know the capabilities and limitations of every machine in his department and should be able to tell new people how to operate them effectively.

6. *Education.*—While it is true that more and more foremen have had college training, a college education is not regarded as a necessary qualification. Some of the country's best foremen have never been to college. Insofar as education is concerned, top management is looking, first, for foremen whose background provides a broad commonsense viewpoint and practical understanding. Although college training helps in the development of these qualities, it is also recognized that such qualities can be the outgrowth of past experience.

7. *Initiative.*—A foreman must be a self-starter. If he is to discharge his responsibility as a manager of a function, he must be capable of taking action necessary to keep production going with only occasional supervision from his superiors. Any foreman who requires constant supervision is not performing the functions of a foreman.

8. *Human interest.*—A foreman should be interested in all things which affect the wellbeing of his employees. This involves personal as well as shop problems because personal problems frequently affect performance on the job. Moreover, the foreman is, oftentimes, the only person to whom employees can go for counsel and advice on problems of this nature. When a worker knows that the foreman has his personal interest at heart, his morale and job interest are greatly stimulated.

9. *Physical and mental requirements.*—It is needless to say that a foreman must have the physical and emotional capacity to carry his responsibilities and perform his duties with the vigor which the job requires.

Finding prospects

Companies generally try to find people within their own organization who can be promoted to the position of foreman whenever a vacancy occurs. They do this because it has a definite bearing on the growth and development of foremen into better supervisors. When a man is promoted from the ranks to the position of foreman, he is given evidence that the company is trying -to follow the policy of "promotion from within." This gives him the feeling that if he does a good job as foreman he may have a chance at some later date to be considered for an even better job. A foreman who feels he can look to his own company for advancement, rather than having to look to a competitor, is able for psychological reasons, to give more of himself to his job and his company. This procedure also helps stimulate job interest on the part of the foreman's employees because they, too, feel that if they do a good job where they are, they may later be advanced to the position of foreman. More and more employees are looking for jobs that offer career opportunities, and as long as a company holds to the policy of promotion from within, workers can feel that their present company offers career possibilities.

What kind of training?

Programs for training foremen take various forms. Among them are: programs designed to prepare candidates for promotion to the job of a foreman; programs designed to stimulate die development of existing foremen so they can do a better job; refresher courses for foremen who have already been trained; and programs designed to train foremen for higher positions in the organization.

The fact that foreman training is so strongly emphasized by industry does not mean that the foreman of today is lacking in capability. On the contrary, most foremen are capable, well-qualified people. However, attitudes of people are constantly changing, new labor relations philosophies are being developed, and new processes and new techniques are being introduced. It is only good business to expose foremen to training sessions which will give them the information necessary to keep abreast of the changing industrial picture. The primary reason why such careful attention has been given to the subject of foremen training in recent years is the long-unfilled need which resulted from the time when it was not felt necessary to train foremen at all. It was felt that this need could be adequately met through supervision of the foreman by his superiors. Here is another example of the fact that industrial philosophies and practices change.

A foreman on the job today already has a certain amount of leadership ability, organizational ability, understanding of people, technical skill, and mechanical ability. These are qualifications he has to possess if he is to hold down his job. He can't get production out on time without them. The question is: Can the foreman's ability to lead and understand people, and organize his shop, be improved with training designed to help him in these areas? The answer is: "Yes." Leaders from both large and small companies agree that training in foremanship can definitely help the foreman to develop his abilities and thereby enable him to do a better job in the plant. In addition, after a foreman has taken a course in leadership training, he needs refresher courses from time to time because under pressure of meeting schedules and deadlines even the most conscientious supervisor forgets or overlooks part of what he already knows. Experience proves that die art of getting things done through people is a subject which supervisors can, with profit, be coached in—*at regular intervals*.

The foreman also needs training in shop organization and in work simplification. There are certain basic principles of good organization which can be applied to most any department Also, new techniques are developed from time to time which permit plant procedures to be simplified with a saving of time and money. Any foreman training program should deal with the subject of shop organization techniques because good organization reduces waste and production costs and improves employee morale.

Solving the problem in small plants

Because of practical considerations, small plants are limited in their ability to develop and promote their own formal training programs for foremen. Nevertheless, many of them consider the need for this training to be of such importance that they are discovering ways and means for making it available in spite of limited resources. In general, small plants are working through one of four general methods.

Cooperation with other small plants.—In areas where a number of small plants are located, arrangements can often be made whereby several plants jointly hire a training specialist who develops a foreman training program designed to fit the particular needs of the cooperating plants. Such projects are financed by the cooperating firms on a joint basis. Arrangements of this type have proved successful in Chicago, Pittsburgh, and Philadelphia. The idea was developed with the help of management consulting firms.

Cooperation with colleges and universities.—Some colleges and universities, in cooperation with small plants, have developed foreman and supervisory training programs designed to meet the needs of plants in their particular areas. These programs are usually offered in connection with adult training courses given by the colleges. Those who attend usually get the benefit of instruction both from college professors who have specialized in training problems and from industrial experts. While there are relatively few such arrangements-at least so far as foremen are concerned-plants that have participated in projects of this type regard them as most successful. An alternative method of training foremen is the home study course. Subjects taught by accredited home study schools include quality control, report writing, safety engineering, and others.

Use of programs developed by larger companies.—Some small plants purchase foreman training programs from larger companies which are in the same general type of business. They use such programs to conduct training sessions under the leadership of someone on their own staff. Some large companies are very generous in letting other companies use their material. While this arrangement has its disadvantages, it has been known to produce desirable results, especially where the directors of such training sessions are skilled in conference leadership techniques. Those who use this arrangement point out that, in the final analysis, foremen will train each other if (1) they have an adequate text upon which to base their discussions, and (2) the leader of the training sessions is gifted in stimulating group discussions in connection with problems which foremen as individuals face on their particular jobs.

Where a small company has a close relationship with one of the larger companies, arrangements can often be made whereby the small plant sends a member of its staff to attend the foreman training course of the large company. That person ultimately returns and serves as an instructor for foremen in his own plant It should he noted, however, that training programs developed for large companies need to be modified if they are used in small plants.

Use of supervisory programs developed by management associations.—Some small plants solve their foreman training problem by making use of the staff facilities of national management associations. The assistance rendered by such organizations to small plants has produced excellent results. Among those associations which have taken an active interest in foremen training are the National Association of Manufacturers, some local Chambers of Commerce, the National Association of Foremen, the Foremen's League, and the American Management Association. These groups offer a variety of services which can and are being utilized by small companies as follows:

1. Some have training specialists who are available to small businesses for the purpose of conducting foremen and supervisory training programs.
2. Some have training specialists available as consultants for the purpose of helping small establishments set up their own training program.
3. Some have foreman training programs of various types which small plants can use in conducting their own training sessions.
4. Some offer a generalized type of foreman training through the use of foremen's clubs. Such clubs are designed to promote a better understanding by the foreman of his responsibilities as a member of management.

Measuring the results

Since a training program for foremen deals with leadership and organizational problems, the results of the training can usually be measured only in terms of the foreman's performance on the job. There is no way to predict from classroom discussions how valuable the training will be to the company. The results of such training, if they are to be of value, must be reflected in the performance records of the foreman's department. If the course has been a success, proof will be found in increased ability to get work out in less time, with less expense, and with fewer employee grievances than previously. While it may take weeks for any results to become apparent, a good foreman training program will help to accomplish this objective. Following are the specific items by which the foreman's performance can be measured to determine what results have been obtained: overtime expense, number of production units which have been rejected, amount of material wasted, number of workers required to get the work out, number of hours the machines are utilized, the number and nature of employee grievances which are filed, and the amount of absenteeism. If the training program has been successful, there should in due time be an improvement in each of the categories listed above.

How top management promotes foreman development

A training program alone is not sufficient to encourage the development of foremen to the maximum extent. After a foreman has completed his training, he wants to see evidence that his job is as important as the training program led him to believe. If he is to be regarded as a part of management, he wants to be given the authority, prestige, and recognition which goes with it. Once he has been given proper recognition, this tends to serve as a constant reminder of the importance of his job and encourages him to make greater efforts toward self-improvement on his own initiative.

There are several ways in which top management can provide the proper recognition to foremen:

Incentive payments.—Many firms have the policy of paying bonuses to their top management in proportion to their salaries, based upon how much profit the company makes each year. By spreading such bonus payments to all levels of management, foremen and other supervisors are made to feel that they really are a part of management and that the more efficiently they run their shops, the greater the chance that their annual bonuses will be increased.

Authority.—It is not enough to spell out the duties and responsibilities of the foreman. He must be given suitable authority. Top management should also make it clear that they will back up the foreman in any decisions that he makes within the scope of his duties and responsibilities. This helps to promote the growth of the foreman because it keeps him alert to the fact that he is, in reality as well as title, a part of management.

Prestige.—Top management can develop a sense of responsibility and job satisfaction in its foremen, by use of the following other devices:

1. A bulletin from the president to all levels of management informing them of any major changes in company policy. It lets the foreman and other supervisors know that the top management prefers for supervisors to get the story direct rather than through the grapevine or the newspapers.
2. Staff sessions called by top management of a small plant for the purpose of getting advice on company problems have proved effective in developing a broader sense of responsibility among foremen.
3. Occasional banquets where all levels of management are invited for getting-acquainted purposes helps to stimulate job enthusiasm on the part of foremen.

A foreman who is properly trained and who enjoys proper recognition of his status is one of the most important people in industry today. The extent to which he develops his abilities to do the job expected of him is, in large measure, dependent upon how much interest top management in the small plant is willing to take in him.

———

MANPOWER ESTIMATES—CARPENTRY

This appendix contains tables which may be used in preparing manpower estimates for carpentry work. The tables do not include provision for loading and hauling materials to the jobsite.

All tables presume average working conditions in terms of weather, skill, crew size, accessibility, and the availability of equipment.

Table D–1. Rough Framing [1]

Description	Unit	Man-hr/unit		
Beams (3–2″ x 8″)	MFBM [2]	40		
Blocking	MFBM	32		
Bridging	100 pairs	5		
Ceiling joists	MFBM	32		
Door bucks	ea.	3		
Floor joists, sills	MFBM	32		
Furring including plugging	1000 linft	32		
Grounds for plaster	1000 linft	48		
Rafters	MFBM	48		
Trusses	ea.	Man-hr assembly	Man-hr placement	Hours hoist time
Span ft 20		2.5	4	8
30		5	8	12
40		12	8	16
50		20	6 [3]	8 [3]
60		24	6 [3]	9 [3]
80		32	6 [3]	11 [3]
Wall frames, plates	MFBM	56		

[1] Typical crew: 1 leader, 8 men.
Minimal crew: 1 leader, 2 men.
[2] Thousand board feet measure.
[3] Assumes use of organizational crane.

Table D-2. Sheathing and Siding [1]

Description	Unit	Man-hr/unit
Roof decking	1000 sq ft	
plywood		24
tongue & groove		32
Siding	1000 sq ft	
corrugated asbestos		32
drop siding		32
narrow bevel		48
plywood		24
shingles		40
Wall sheathing	1000 sq ft	
Bldg paper		16
fiber board		24
tongue & groove		24
plywood		16

[1] Typical crew: 1 leader, 4 men.

Table D-3. Flooring [1]

Description	Unit	Man-hr/unit
Linoleum	1000 sq ft	32
Soft tile	1000 sq ft	
cemented		24
nailed		32
Wood floors	1000 sq ft	
Finish floor		
hardwood		32
softwood		24
Subfloor		
plywood		16
tongue & groove		24

[1] Typical crew: 1 leader, 4 men.

Table D-4. Insulation [1]

Description	Unit	Man-hr/unit
Acoustic	1000 sq ft	
Quilt		8
Strip		24
Thermal	1000 sq ft	
Board		
ceiling		24
floor		8
roof		16
wall		32
Foil alone		16
Rigid foam		32
Rock wool		
batts		24
loose		16

[1] Typical crew: 1 leader, 8 men.

Table D-5. Finish Carpentry [1]

Description	Unit	Man-hr/unit
Baseboard (2 member)	1000 linft	72
Ceilings	1000 sq ft	
cemented tile		32
panel w/suspension		72
plasterboard (including tape)[2]		64
wood		48
Door frame, trim	ea.	2.5
Installing prefab. closets	ea.	16
Molding (chair)	1000 linft	48
Plasterboard (complete)	1000 sq ft	110
Setting kitchen cabinets	ea.	1.5
Sliding door w/pocket	ea.	8
Shelving	1000 sq ft	64
Stairs		
closed stringer, built on job	story	16
closed stringer, prefab.	story	8
open stringer	story	24
Walls	1000 sq ft	
plasterboard (including tape)		48
plywood		80
Wood frame, trim	ea.	3

[1] Typical crew: 1 leader, 8 men.
[2] Includes installation of furring strips when necessary.

Table D-6. Wood Door Installation [1]

Description	Unit	Man-hr/unit
Caulking (w/gun)	1000 linft	16
Doors w/hardware	ea.	
exterior [2]		2
interior [2]		1.5
manual sliding (including tracks)		8
motorized sliding [3]		56
overhead (including machinery)		16
screendoors		1.5
Weatherstripping	ea. opening	1.5

[1] Typical crew: 1 leader, 4 men.
[2] For double doors add 50% to labor estimates.
[3] Includes tracks and all necessary machinery, with control equipment.

Table D-7. Wood Window Installation [1]

Description	Unit	Man-hr/unit
Caulking (w/gun)	1000 linft	16
Screens	ea.	1.5
Weatherstripping	ea. opening	1.5
Windows (avg 20 sq ft)	ea.	
casement		1.5
double hung		2.5
jalousie		2.5
louvers		4
skylight		8
sliding		2.5
Venetian blinds	ea.	1

[1] Typical crew: 1 leader, 4 men.

Table D-8. Built-Up Roofing, Insulation and Flashing [1] (pitch 1/2"—3"/ft)

Description	Unit	Man-hr/unit
Flashing	1000 linft	60
Insulation	1000 sq ft	25
Roofing	1000 sq ft	
2 ply		12
3 ply		20
4 ply		25
5 ply		30

[1] Typical crew: 1 leader, 6 men.
Table includes melting asphalt, laying felt, mopping, and laying gravel.

Table D-9. Roll Roofing [1] (pitch at least 2"/ft)

Description	Unit	Man-hr/unit
Asphaltic aluminum (including primer)	1000 sq ft	18
Canvas (including 2 coats paint)	1000 sq ft	25
Paper (plain) & felt	1000 sq ft	7

[1] Typical crew: 1 leader, 6 men.
Table includes cleaning deck, applying prime coat, and laying rolls.

Table D-10. Shingle Roofing [1] (pitch at least 3"/ft)

Description	Unit	Man-hr/unit
Asbestos	1000 sq ft	45
Asphalt	1000 sq ft	30
Metal	1000 sq ft	50
Slate	1000 sq ft	55
Wood	1000 sq ft	35

[1] Typical crew: 1 leader, 4 men.
Table includes placing and nailing.

Table D-11. Metal, Asbestos-Cement and Tile Roofing [1] (pitch at least 3"/ft)

Description	Unit	Man-hr/unit
Asbestos-cement	1000 sq ft	
metal purlins		45
wood purlins		35
Metal — corrugated & V-crimp	1000 sq ft	
metal purlins		36
wood purlins		18
Tile	1000 sq ft	
clay		55
metal		60

[1] Typical crew: 1 leader, 5 men.
Table includes placing, caulking, drilling, and fastening materials.

Table D-12. Pile Bracing and Capping [1]

Description	Unit	Man-hr/unit
Bracing [2]	ea.	
diagonal		0.8
horizontal		1
Capping wood	1000 linft	100

[1] Typical crew: 1 leader, 6 men.
[2] Table based on 4 in x 10 in x 4 ft bracing members.
Pile bracing includes cutting, drilling, handling, and fastening materials.

Table D-13. Pier Framing [1]

Description	Unit	Man-hr/unit
Bridging	1000 linft	40
Bull rail	1000 linft	60
Bumper	1000 linft	36
4" deck	1000 sq ft	20
Stringers	MFBM [2]	200
2" wearing surface	1000 sq ft	16

[1] Typical crew: 1 leader, 10 men.
[2] 1000 board-foot measure.
Installation of pier framing includes the cutting, drilling, handling, and fastening of stringers, bridging, all decking, rails, and bumpers.

Table D-14. Deck Hardware [1]

Description	Unit	Man-hr/unit
Bits	ea.	3
Bollards	ea.	4
Chocks	ea.	3
Cleats	ea.	2
Pad eyes	ea.	1

[1] Typical crew: 1 leader, 4 men.
Installation of deck hardware includes required drilling, handling, and fastening of bits, bollards, chocks, cleats, and pad eyes.

ABBREVIATIONS AND SYMBOLS
CONTENTS

Page

—————

ABBREVIATIONS AND SYMBOLS

1.   Abbreviations

The following abbreviations in connection with lumber are used by the carpenter:

AD - - - - - - - - - -air-dried
al - - - - - - - - - - -all length
av - - - - - - - - - - -average
avw - - - - - - - - -average width
avl - - - - - - - - -average length
bd - - - - - - - - - -board
bd ft - - - - - - - -board foot
bdl- - - - - - - - - -bundle
bev - - - - - - - - -beveled
bm - - - - - - - - -board (foot) measure
btr - - - - - - - - - -better
clg- - - - - - - - - -ceiling
clr - - - - - - - - - -clear
CM - - - - - - - -center matched; that is, tongue-and-groove joints are made along the center of
                    the edge of the piece
Com - - - - - - -common
Csg - - - - - - - - -casing
Ctg - - - - - - - - -crating
cu ft- - - - - - - -cubic foot
D & CM - - - - - -dressed (one or two sides) and center matched
D & M - - - - - -dressed and matched; that is, dressed one or two sides and tongue and
                    grooved on the edges. The match may be center or standard
DS - - - - - - - - -drop siding
D & SM - - - - - -dressed (one or two sides) and standard matched
D 2S & CM- - -dressed two sides and center matched
D 2S & M- - - - -dressed two sides and (center of standard) matched
D 2S & SM- - -dressed two sides and standard matched
Dim - - - - - - - -dimension
E- - - - - - - - - - -edge
FAS- - - - - - - -firsts and seconds, a combined grade of the two upper grades of hardwoods
fbk- - - - - - - - - -flat back
fcty - - - - - - - -factory (lumber)
FG - - - - - - - - -flat grain
Flg - - - - - - - - -flooring
fok- - - - - - - - - -free of knots
Frm - - - - - - - -framing
ft - - - - - - - - - - -foot or feet
Hdl - - - - - - - - -handle (stock)
Hdwd- - - - - - -hardwood
Hrt - - - - - - - - -heart
Hrtwd - - - - - -heartwood
in - - - - - - - - - -inch or inches

KD - - - - - - - - - -kiln-dried
kd - - - - - - - - - -knocked down
lbr - - - - - - - - - -lumber
lgr - - - - - - - - - -longer
lgth - - - - - - - - -length
linft - - - - - - - -linear foot, that is, 12 inches
LR- - - - - - - - - -log run
Lr MCO - - - - - -log run, mill culls out
M - - - - - - - - - -thousand
MFBM - - - - - - -thousand (feet) board measure
MCO - - - - - - - -mill culls out
Merch - - - - - - -merchantable
MR - - - - - - - - -mill run
msm - - - - - - - -thousand (feet) surface measure
mw - - - - - - - - -mixed width
No- - - - - - - - - -number
1s & 2s - - - - - -ones and twos, a combined grade of the hardwood grades of firsts and sec-
                        onds
Ord - - - - - - - - -order
P- - - - - - - - - - -planed
Pat - - - - - - - - -pattern
Pky - - - - - - - - -picky
Pln - - - - - - - - -plain, as in plain sawed
Pn- - - - - - - - - -partition
Qtd - - - - - - - - -quartered (with reference to hardwoods)
rd - - - - - - - - - -round
rdm - - - - - - -random
res - - - - - - - -resawed
rf g - - - - - - - -roofing
Rfrs- - - - - - - -roofers
rip - - - - - - - -ripped
rl - - - - - - - - - -random length
rw - - - - - - - - -random width
S & E - - - - - -surfaced one side and one edge
S2S & M - - - -surfaced two sides and standard or center matched
S2S & SM - - - -.surfaced two sides and standard matched
Sap - - - - - - -sapwood
S1E - - - - - - -surfaced one edge
S1S1E - - - - -surf aced one side and one edge
S1S2E - - - - -surfaced one side and two edges
S2E - - - - - - -surfaced two edges
S4S - - - - - - -.surfaced four sides
S & CM - - - - -surfaced one or two sides and center matched
S & M - - - - - -surfaced and matched; that is, surfaced one or two sides and tongued and
                        grooved on the edges. The match may be center or standard.
S & SM - - - - -surfaced one or two sides and standard matched
S2S & CM - - - -surfaced two sides and center matched
Sap - - - - - - -sapwood
SB - - - - - - - -standard bead
Sd- - - - - - - - -seasoned

```
Sdg      - - - - - - - -siding
Sel  - - - - - - - - -select
SESd- - - - - - - -square-edge siding
sf  - - - - - - - - - -surface foot; that is, an area of 1 square foot
Stfwd- - - - - - -softwood
ShD   - - - - - - - -shipping dry
Ship  - - - - - - -shiplap
Sm  - - - - - - - - -standard matched
sm   - - - - - - - - -surface measure
snd - - - - - - - - -sap no defect
snd - - - - - - - -sound
sq - - - - - - - - - -square
sq E  - - - - - - - -square edge
sq E & S  - - - - -square edge and sound
sqrs- - - - - - - -squares
Std - - - - - - - - -standard
stk- - - - - - - - -stock
SW - - - - - - - - -sound wormy
T & G  - - - - - - -tongued and grooved
TB & S  - - - - - -top, bottom, and sides
tbrs - - - - - - - -timbers
VG  - - - - - - - - -vertical grain
wal - - - - - - - - -wider, all length
wdr - - - - - - - - -wider
wt - - - - - - - - - -weight
wth - - - - - - - -width
```

—————

2. Symbols

Symbols commonly used in carpentry are given below. For additional information on the various symbols used in construction plans and blueprints, refer to TM 5-704.

a. *Architectural*

Tile -

Earth -

Plaster -

Sheet metal -

Built-in cabinet -

Outside door: Brick wall - - - - - - - - - - - - - - - -

Frame wall - - - - - - - - - - - - - -

Inside door: Frame wall - - - - - - - - - - - - - - - - - -

Brick -

Firebrick -

Concrete -

Cast concrete block -

Insulation : Loose fill -

Board or quilts - - - - - - - - - - - - - - - - -

Cut stone -

Ashlar -

Shingles (siding) -

Wood, rough -

Wood, finished -

Cased or arched openings - - - - - - - - - - - - - - - -

Single caseinent window - - - - - - - - - - - - - - - -

Double hung windows - - - - - - - - - - - - - - - - - - -

Double casement window - - - - - - - - - - - - - - - -

b. *Plumbing*

Bathtubs:

    Corner - - - - - - - - - -

    Free standing - - - - - -

Floor drain- - - - - - - - - -

Shower drain - - - - - - - -

Hot-water tank- - - - - - - -   H. W. T.

Grease trap - - - - - - - - -

Hose bibb or sill cock - - -

Lavatories:

    Pedestal - - - - - - - - -

    Wall-hung - - - - - - - -

    Corner. - - - - - - - - - -

Toilets:

    Tank - - - - - - - - - - -

    Flush valve - - - - - - - -

Urinals:

    Stall-type - - - - - - - - -

    Wall-hung. - - - - - - - -

Laundry trays - - - - - -

Built-in shower - - - - -

Shower - - - - - - - - - -

Sinks:

    Single drain board.

    Double drain board.

C. *Electrical*

Pull switch - - - - - - - - - -   Ceiling outlet - - - - - - -

Single-pole switch - - - - - S_1 Wall bracket - - - - - - -

Double-pole switch - - - - - S_2 Single convenience outlet - - - - - - - - - - - - -

Triple-pole switch - - - - - - S_3 Double convenience outlet - - - - - - - - - - - - -

Buzzer - - - - - - - - - - - -   Ceiling outlet. gas & electric - - - - - - - - - - - - -

Floor outlet - - - - - - - - -   Motor - - - - - - - - - - -

Bell - - - - - - - - - - - - - -   Light outlet with wir-
ing and switches indi-

Drop cord - - - - - - - - - -   cated - - - - - - - - - - - -

GLOSSARY OF CARPENTRY AND BUILDING CONSTRUCTION TERMS

TABLE OF CONTENTS

GLOSSARY OF CARPENTY AND BUILDING CONSTRUCTION TERMS

Anchor - Irons of special form used to fasten together timbers or masonry.

Anchor bolts - Bolt which fastens columns, girders, or other members to concrete or masonry.

Backing - The bevel on the top edge of a hip rafter that allows the roofing board to fit the top of the rafter without leaving a triangular space between it and the lower side of the roof covering.

Balloon frame - The lightest and most economical form of construction, in which the studding and corner posts are set up in continuous lengths from first-floor line or sill to the roof plate.

Baluster- A small pillar or column used to support a rail.

Balustrade - A series of balusters connected by a rail, generally used for porches, balconies, and the like.

Band - A low, flat molding.

Base - The bottom of a column; the finish of a room at the junction of the walls and floor.

Batten (cleat) - A narrow strip of board used to fasten several pieces together.

Batter board - A temporary framework used to assist in locating the corners when laying a foundation.

Batter pile - Pile driven at an angle to brace a structure against lateral thrust.

Beam - An inclusive term for joists, girders, rafters, and purlins.

Bedding - A filling of mortar, putty, or other substance in order to secure a firm bearing.

Belt course - A horizontal board across or around a building, usually made of a flat member and a molding.

Bent -A single vertical framework consisting of horizontal and vertical members supporting the deck of a bridge or pier.

Bevel board (pitch board) - A board used in framing a roof or stairway to lay out bevels.

Board - Lumber less than 2 inches thick.

Board foot - The equivalent of a board 1 foot square and 1 inch thick.

Boarding in - The process of nailing boards on the outside studding of a house.

Bollard - Steel or cast iron post to which large ships are tied.

Braces - Pieces fitted and firmly fastened to two others at any angle in order to strengthen the angle thus treated.

Bracket - A projecting support for a shelf or other structure.

Break joints - To arrange joints so that they do not come directly under or over the joints of adjoining pieces, as in shingling, siding, etc.

Bridging - Pieces fitted in pairs from the bottom of one floor joist to the top of adjacent joists, and crossed to distribute the floor load; sometimes pieces of width equal to the joists and fitted neatly between them.

Building paper - Cheap, thick paper, used to insulate a building before the siding or roofing is put on; sometimes placed between double floors.

Built-up member - A single structural component made from several pieces fastened together.

Built-up timber - A timber made of several pieces fastened together, and forming one of larger dimension.

Carriages - The supports or the steps and risers of a flight of stairs.

Casement - A window in which the sash opens upon hinges.

Casing - The trimming around a door or window opening, either outside or inside, or the finished lumber around a post or beam, etc.

Ceiling - Narrow, matched boards; sheathing of the surfaces that inclose the upper side of room.

Center-hung sash - A sash hung on its centers so that it swings on a horizontal axis.

Chamfer - A beveled surface cut upon the corner of a piece of wood.

Checks - Splits or cracks in a board, ordinarily caused by seasoning.

Chock - Heavy timber fitted between fender piles along wheel guard of a pier or wharf.

Chord - The principal member of a truss on either the top or bottom.

Clamp - A mechanical device used to hold two or more pieces together.

Clapboards - A special form of outside covering of a house; siding.

Cleats - Metal arms extending horizontally from a relatively low base used for securing small ships, tugs, and work boats.

Column - A square, rectangular, or cylindrical support for roofs, ceilings, and so forth, composed of base, shaft, and capital.

Combination frame - A combination of the principal features of the full and balloon frames.

Concrete - An artificial building material made by mixing cement and sand with gravel, broken stone, or other aggregate, and sufficient water to cause the cement to set and bind the entire mass.

Conductors - Pipes for conducting water from a roof to the ground or to a receptacle or drain; downspout.

Cornice - The molded projection which finishes the top of the wall of a building.

Counterflashings - Strips of metal used to prevent water from entering the top edge of the vertical side of a roof flashing; they also allow expansion and contraction without danger of breaking the flashing.

Cross brace - Bracing with two intersecting diagonals.

Deadening - Construction intended to prevent the passage of sound.

Decking - Heavy plank floor of a pier or bridge.

Diagonal - Inclined member of a truss or bracing system used for stiffening and wind bracing.

Drip - The projection of a window sill or water table to allow the water to drain clear of the side of the house below it.

Fascia - A flat member of a cornice or other finish, generally the board of the cornice to whic the gutter is fastened.

Fender pile - Outside row of piles that protects a pier or wharf from damage by ships.

Fitter - Piece used to fill space between two surfaces.

Flashing - The material used and the process of making watertight the roof intersections and other exposed places on the outside of the house.

Flue - The opening in a chimney through which smoke passes.

Flush - Adjacent surfaces even, or in same plane (with reference to two structural pieces).

Footing - An enlargement at the lower end of a wall, pier, or column, to distribute the load.

Footing form - A wooden or steel structure, placed around the footing that will hold the concrete to the desired shape and size.

Foundation - That part of a building or wall which supports the superstructure.

Frame - The surrounding or inclosing woodwork of windows, doors, etc., and the timber skeleton of building.

Framing - The rough timber structure of a building, including interior and exterior walls, floor, roof, and ceilings.

Full frame - The old fashioned mortised-and-tenoned frame, in which every joint was mortised and tenoned. Rarely used at the present time.

Furring - Narrow strips of board nailed upon the walls and ceilings to form a straight surface upon which to lay the laths or other finish.

Gable - The vertical triangular end of a building from the eaves to the apex of the roof.

Gage - A tool used by carpenters to strike a line parallel to the edge of a board.

Gambrel - A symmetrical roof with two different pitches or slopes on each side.

Girder - A timber used to support wall beams or joists.

Girt (ribband) - The horizontal member of the walls of a full or combination frame house which supports the floor joists or is flush with the top of the joists.

Grade - The horizontal ground level of a building or structure.

Groove - A long hollow channel cut by a tool, into which a piece fits or in which it works. Two special types of grooves are the *dado,* a rectangular groove cut across the full width of a piece, and the *housing,* a groove cut at any angle with the grain and part way across a piece. Dados are used in sliding doors, window frames, etc.; housings are used for framing stair risers and threads in a string.

Ground - A strip of wood assisting the plasterer in making a straight wall and in giving a place to which the finish of the room may be nailed.

Hanger - Vertical-tension member supporting a load.

Header - A short joist into which the common joists are framed around or over an opening.

Headroom - The clear space between floor line and ceiling, as in a stairway.

Heel of a rafter - The end or foot that rests on the wall plate.

Hip roof - A roof which slopes up toward the center from all sides, necessitating a hip rafter at each corner.

Jack rafter - A short rafter framing between the wall plate; a hip rafter.

Jamb - The side piece or post of an opening; sometimes applied to the door frame.

Joint-butt - Squared ends or ends and edges adjoining each other:

  Dovetail - Joint made by cutting pins the shape of dovetails which fit between dovetail upon another piece.

  Drawboard - A mortise-and-tenon joint with holes so bored that when a pin is driven through, the joint becomes tighter.

  Fished - An end butt splice strengthened by pieces nailed on the sides.

  Glue - A joint held together with glue.

  Halved - A joint made by cutting half the wood away from each piece so as to bring the sides flush.

  Housed - A joint in which a piece is grooved to receive the piece which is to form the other part of the joint.

  Lap - A joint of two pieces lapping over each other.

  Mortised - A joint made by cutting a hole or mortise, in one piece, and a tenon, or piece to fit the hole, upon the other.

  Rub - A flue joint made by carefully fitting the edges together, spreading glue between them, and rubbing the pieces back and forth until the pieces are well rubbed together.

  Scarfed - A timber spliced by cutting various shapes of shoulders, or jogs, which fit each other.

Joists - Timbers supporting the floorboards.

Kerf - The cut made by a saw.

Knee brace - A corner brace, fastened at an angle from wall stud to rafter, stiffening a wood or steel frame to prevent angular movement.

Laths - Narrow strips to support plastering.

Lattice - Crossed wood, iron plate, or bars.

Ledgerboard - The support for the second-floor joists of a balloon-frame house, or for similar uses; ribband.

Level - A term describing the position of a line or plane when parallel to the surface of still water; an instrument or tool used in testing for horizontal and vertical surfaces, and in determining differences of elevation.

*Lintel (cap -)*A horizontal structural member spanning an opening, and supporting a wall load.

Lookout - The end of a rafter, or the construction which projects beyond the sides of a house to support the eaves; also the projecting timbers at the gables which support the verge boards.

Louver - A kind of window, generally in peaks of gables and the tops of towers, provided with horizontal slots which exclude rain and snow and allow ventilation.

Lumber - Sawed parts of a log such as boards, planks, scantling, and timber.

Matching, or tonguing and grooving - The method used in cutting the edges of a board to make a tongue on one edge and a groove on the other.

Meeting rail - The bottom rail of the upper sash of a double-hung window. Sometimes called the check-rail.

Member - A single piece in a structure, complete in itself.

Miter - The joint formed by two abutting pieces meeting at an angle.

Molding Base - The molding on the top of a baseboard.

> *Bed* – A molding used to cover the joint between the plancier and frieze (horizontal decorative band around the wall of a room); also used as a base molding upon heavy work, and sometimes as a member of a cornice.

> *Lip* - A molding with a lip which overlaps the piece against which the back of the molding rests.

> *Picture* - A molding shaped to form a support for picture hooks, often placed at some distance from the ceiling upon the wall to form the lower edge of the frieze.

> *Rake* - The cornice upon the gable edge of a pitch roof, the members of which are made to fit those of the molding of the horizontal eaves.

Mortise - The hole which is to receive a tenon, or any hole cut into or through a piece by a chisel; generally of rectangular shape.

Mullion - The construction between the openings of a window frame to accommodate two or more windows.

Muntin - The vertical member between two panels of the same piece of panel work. The vertical sash-bars separating the different panels of glass.

Newel - The principal post of the foot of a staircase; also the central support of a winding flight of stairs.

Nosing - The part of a stair tread which projects over the riser, or any similar projection; a term applied to the rounded edge of a board.

Pad eyes - Metal rings mounted vertically on a plate for tying small vessels.

Partition - A permanent interior wall which serves to divide a building into rooms.

Pier-(a) Timber, concrete, or masonry supports for girders, posts, or arches. (b) Intermediate supports for adjacent ends of two bridge spans. (c) Structure extending outward from shore into water used as a dock for ships.

*Piers-*Masonry supports, set independently of the main foundation.

Pilaster - A portion of a square column, usually set within or against a wall.

Piles - Long posts driven into the soil in swampy locations or whenever it is difficult to secure a firm foundation, upon which the footing course of masonry or other timbers are laid.

Piling - Large timbers or poles driven into the ground or the bed of a stream to make a firm foundation.

Pitch - Inclination or slope, as for roofs or stairs, or the rise divided by the span.

Pitch board - A board sawed to the exact shape formed by the stair tread, riser, and slope of the stairs and used to lay out the carriage and stringers.

Plan - A horizontal geometrical section of a building, showing the walls, doors, windows, stairs, chimneys, columns, etc.

Plank - A wide piece of sawed timber, usually 1 1/2 to 4 1/2 inches thick and 6 inches or more wide.

Plaster - A mixture of lime, hair, and sand, or of lime, cement, and sand, used to cover outside and inside wall surfaces.

Plate - The top horizontal piece of the walls of a frame building upon which the roof rests.

Plate cut - The cut in a rafter which rests upon the plate; sometimes called the seat cut.

Plow - To cut a groove running in the same direction as the grain of the wood.

Plumb cut - Any cut made in a vertical plane; the vertical cut at the top end of a rafter.

Ply - A term used to denote a layer or thickness of building or roofing paper as two-ply, three-ply, etc.

Porch - An ornamental entrance way.

Post - A timber set on end to support a wall, girder, or other member of the structure.

Pulley stile - The member of a window frame which contains the pulleys and between which the edges of the sash slide.

Purlin - A timber supporting several rafters at one or more points, or the roof sheeting directly.

Rabbet or rebate - A corner cut out of an edge of a piece of wood.

Rafter - The beams that slope from the ridge of a roof to the eaves and make up the main body of the roof's framework.

Rafters, common - Those which run square with the plate and extend to the ridge.

    Cripple - Those which cut between valley and hip rafters.

    Hip - Those extending from the outside angle of the plates toward the apex of the roof.

    Jacks - Those square with the plate and intersecting the hip rafter.

    Valley - Those extending from an inside angle of the plates toward the ridge or center line of the house.

Rail - The horizontal members of a balustrade or panel work.

Rake - The trim of a building extending in an oblique line, as rake dado or molding.

Return - The continuation of a molding or finish of any kind in a different direction.

Ribband - (See Ledgerboard.)

Ridge - The top edge or corner formed by the intersection of two roof surfaces.

Ridge cut - (See Plumb cut.)

Rise - The vertical distance through which anything rises, as the rise of a roof or stair.

Riser - The vertical board between two treads of a flight of stairs.

Roofing - The material put on a roof to make it wind and waterproof.

Rubble - Roughly broken quarry stone.

Rubble masonry - Uncut stone, used for rough work, foundations, backing, and the like.

Run - The length of the horizontal projection of a piece such as a rafter when in position.

Saddle board - The finish of the ridge of a pitch-roof house. Sometimes called comb board.

Sash - The framework which holds the glass in a window.

Sawing, plain - Lumber sawed regardless of the grain, the log simply squared and sawed to the desired thickness; sometimes called slash or bastard sawed.

Scab - A short piece of lumber used to splice, or to prevent movement of two other pieces.

Scaffold or staging - A temporary structure or platform enabling workmen to reach high places.

Scale - A short measurement used as a proportionate part of a larger dimension. The scale of a drawing is expressed as 14 inch = 1 foot.

Scantling - Lumber with a cross-section ranging from 2 by 4 inches to 4 by 4 inches.

Scarfing - A joint between two pieces of wood which allows them to be spliced lengthwise.

Scotia - A hollow molding used as a part of a cornice, and often under the nosing of a stair tread.

Scribing - The marking of a piece of wood to provide for the fitting of one of its surfaces to the irregular surface of another.

Seat cut or plate cut - The cut at the bottom end of a rafter to allow it to fit upon the plate.

Seat of a rafter -The horizontal cut upon the bottom end of a rafter which rests upon the top of the plate.

Section - A drawing showing the kind, arrangement, and proportions of the various parts of a structure. It is assumed that the structure is cut by a plane, and the section is the view gained by looking in one direction.

Shakes -Imperfections in timber caused during the growth of the timber by high winds or imperfect conditions of growth.

Sheathing -Wall boards, roofing boards; generally applied to narrow boards laid with a space between them, according to the length of a shingle exposed to weather.

Sheathing paper -The paper used under siding or shingles to insulate in the house; building papers.

Siding -The outside finish between the casings.

Sills -The horizontal timbers of a house which either rest upon the masonry foundations or, in the absence of such, form the foundations.

Sizing - Working material to the desired size; a coating of glue, shellac, or other substance applied to a surface to prepare it for painting or other method of finish.

Sleeper - A timber laid on the ground to support a floor joist.

Span - The distance between the bearings of a timber or arch.

Specifications - The written or printed directions regarding the details of a building or other construction.

Splice - Joining of two similar members in a straight line.

Square - A tool used by mechanics to obtain accuracy; a term applied to a surface including 100 square feet.

Stairs, box -Those built between walls, and usually with no support except the wall.

Standing finish - Term applied to the finish of the openings and the base, and all other finish work necessary for the inside.

Stringer - A long horizontal timber in a structure supporting a floor.

Stucco -A fine plaster used for interior decoration and fine work; also for rough outside wall coverings.

Stud - An upright beam in the framework of a building.

Studding - The framework of a partition or the wall of a house; usually referred to as 2 by 4@s.

Sub floor - A wood floor which is laid over the floor joists and on which the finished floor is laid.

Threshold - The beveled piece over which the door swings; sometimes called a carpet strip.

Tie beam (collar beam) - A beam so situated that it ties the principal rafters of a roof together and prevents them from thrusting the plate out of line.

Timber - Lumber with cross-section over 4 by 6 inches, such as posts, sills, and girders.

Tin shingle - A small piece of tin used in flashing and repairing a shingle roof.

Top plate - Piece of lumber supporting ends of rafters.

To the iveather - A term applied to the projecting of shingles or siding beyond the course above.

Tread - The horizontal part of a step.

Trim - A term sometimes applied to outside or interior finished woodwork and the finish around openings.

Trimmer -The beam or floor joist into which a header is framed.

Trimming - Putting the inside and outside finish and hardware upon a building.

Truss - Structural framework of triangular units for supporting loads over long spans.

Valleys - The internal angle formed by the two slopes of a roof.

Verge boards - The boards which serve as the eaves finish on the gable end of a building.

Vestibule - An entrance to a house; usually inclosed.

Wainscoting - Matched boarding or panel work covering the lower portion of a wall.

Wale - A horizontal beam.

Wash - The slant upon a sill, capping, etc., to allow the water to run off easily.

Water table - The finish at the bottom of a house which carries water away from the foundation.

Wharf - A structure that provides berthing space for vessels, to facilitate loading and discharge of cargo.

Wind ("i" pronounced as in "kind") - A term used to describe the surface of a board when twisted (winding) or when resting upon two diagonally opposite corners, if laid upon a perfectly flat surface.

Wooden brick - Piece of seasoned wood, made the size of a brick, and laid where it is necessary to provide a nailing space in masonry walls.

CPSIA information can be obtained
at www.ICGtesting.com
Printed in the USA
BVHW010159120522
636869BV00009B/143

9 781731 817792